A JOURNEY THROUGH GRIEF, LOSS, HOPE, & RECOVERY

HOW FAITH GIVES YOU THE FREEDOM TO CHOOSE JOY

DEB KING

ISBN: 979-8-9868476-0-3 EBook

979-8-9868476-1-0 Hardback

979-8-9868476-2-7 Paperback

CONTENTS

This book is dedicated to my daughters Candace and Nicole. We have walked together through life facing loss, grief, hope, and choosing to find joy. Their love of life, faith in God, and unfailing support have made them a rock of encouragement and love for me on the mountain tops and in the valleys.

1   The Spirit of the Sovereign Lord is on me,
      because the Lord has anointed me
      to proclaim good news to the poor.
      He has sent me to bind up the brokenhearted,
      to proclaim freedom for the captives
      and release from darkness for the prisoners,

2 to proclaim the year of the Lord's favor
      and the day of vengeance of our God,
      to comfort all who mourn,

3 and provide for those who grieve in Zion—
      to bestow on them a crown of beauty
      instead of ashes,
      the oil of joy
      instead of mourning,
      and a garment of praise
      instead of a spirit of despair.
      They will be called oaks of righteousness,
      a planting of the Lord
      for the display of his splendor.

                    Isaiah 61: 1-3 (NIV)

INTRODUCTION

"Into each life some rain must fall,
some days must be dark and dreary. "
–Henry Wadsworth Longfellow

This poem is well-established, and I'm guessing that if you were not currently in a dark and rainy season, you might not have this book in your hand. When grief comes into our lives, we naturally desire to run from it. Instead, God desires us to run to Him.

The road through your grief may look dark as you begin to walk it, but along the way, you will find that God has given you the tools you need to bring light into the darkness. Even better, you'll find that He is walking right beside you.

If that sounds too good to be true, let me reassure you. I'm not talking about something I've never experienced. Neither am I alone in my experience of the peace and joy that can come directly from God when we choose to walk that dark road with Him.

My youngest daughter was three when I watched them wrap her bed in padding. The doctors told me that a bump to her head or torso could cause her to bleed to death internally. I spent that night by her side, pleading, arguing, and rationalizing with God about this little girl.

"God, that's my baby girl!"

But by the night's end, God and I had an understanding. She was His, not mine. He was her Father, and she was on loan to me. He was God; I was not. So the question He asked me in the darkness, with the monitors beeping rhythmically in the background, was, *"Do you trust Me? Do you believe I have the best plan for her?"* And by morning, I had my answer. *"Yes."*

I didn't have to like it. I didn't have to want it. But I was at peace with whatever He decided.

The Dark Road

Grief, whether it comes from sickness, death, divorce, loss of a dream, or any other source—whether caused by ourselves or by someone else—is something we will all experience at some point. And as meaningful as whatever caused your grief is, I have found that the thing that matters more is what you do with it.

I had two friends who went through very similar divorces within a year of each other. Both husbands left suddenly, abandoned their children, moved on to new women immediately, and did their best to turn people against their ex-wives. Both women were devastated, heartbroken, impoverished, and afraid. But the similarities end there.

One woman moved forward through her grief, dealing with the fallout in her children and her own heart, and is now a women's pastor, using her experiences to help others. In her grief, she made choices that led her toward healing, peace, and freedom. The other stayed stuck, became bitter, turned away from God, and now struggles with severe anxiety and depression. In her grief, she made choices that compounded her hurt and anger and led her life into a downward spiral of more regret and more pain. As I watched both of them, I kept seeing that the one who eventually experienced healing ran *to* God with her grief, while the other friend ran away from Him.

During my life, I have had to walk down the road of grief with God more than once. Traumatic experiences including an abusive marriage that ended in divorce early in my adult life led me into addiction. Two years after going through treatment, I married Marvin and was married to him for fourteen years. Marvin had nine heart attacks in the last six years of his life. After he passed, I was a widow for nine years before I married Steve. I lost my mother and father within a few years of each other, and my father-in-law passed away just as Steve was beginning his battle with cancer. After a nine-month battle, Steve also passed. Throughout the years, there have been successes and failures; both have had their cost and reason to grieve.

In all these experiences, I have had to wrestle through the same question with God: Do you trust Me? Over and over again, I have learned to say yes. And repeatedly, God has proved to me that He is faithful. Through all this, He has given me a passion for helping others get through the hard places and finding peace amidst excruciating pain, heartache, and joy.

Freedom to Choose

I don't know if your pain was your fault or someone else's, but I know that it can be hard to feel that you have the choice to stand up under the weight of it. But I'm here to be a voice calling in the darkness to you. You have the freedom to choose!

You can choose to get up when you're down, to move

when you feel frozen by fear, to be strong when you are challenged by your circumstances, to be tenacious when you're tired of being strong, to love even when you feel empty, and to give when you think you have nothing of value left to give. When you reach the end of yourself, God steps in and gives you all you need to go on. He provides all you need to succeed, get up, and love more. He is calling you to Himself, where you can become free to focus on Him instead of the storm.

In this book, I want to help you find the road to God in your grief. I will tell you my story... This story is about the loss of family, hopes, and dreams. It's a story of being widowed twice, broken dreams, and blended families. It's a story of how life sometimes turns away from where you thought it was going or wanted it to go. It's a story of the faithfulness of my Heavenly Father through all of it. And it's a story of how God, even in my grief, worked out His plan—the best plan—for my life. Take it from me; this dark road that life takes us down can seem unending, but with God, there is an end to the darkness.

1

WHAT IS GRIEF?

Grief is a strong emotion, which can be overwhelming no matter why someone is grieving. Your sadness may stem from the loss of a loved one, the diagnosis of a terminal illness, the end of a marriage, or any other circumstance. Grief can leave you feeling numb, removed from everyday life, and unable to move forward. You may feel that your grief puts a wall between you and everybody else. It can feel as though the weight of grief has settled on your chest, preventing you from catching your breath.

Grief is a natural reaction to loss. It is both a personal and a universal experience. Your individual experience of grief won't be exactly like anybody else's. It will be influenced by your personality, culture, and the nature of your loss. Even then, everyone grieves differently. Some examples of loss are the death of a loved one, the loss of a job, becoming a victim of theft, the ending of a significant relationship, or the loss of independence through disability.

When grieving, you must realize that you can't control the process. Grief comes in varying stages, and it's wise to prepare yourself to go through all of them. Understanding grief can help you be ready for the emotions you feel, and also help when you're talking to supportive friends and family.

People sometimes spend years trying to resolve their emotional pain, especially if there are complicated issues like feelings of guilt for the death of a loved one or the loss of a spouse with longstanding health or addiction issues. But even without these complications, the grieving process can take months or years. Generally, the pain diminishes gradually as you adapt to life without the person or relationship you are mourning.

Working through grief is essential to moving forward —and God wants us to move forward so that we can walk into the future He has planned for us.

Every Grief Is Different

There are many different types of grief. Each of them will have commonalities with the other, and each will also have things that are unique to that form of loss. Of course, a final loss will be different than a loss that still has the possibility of recovery. But each of them will affect our hearts, our bodies, our minds, and our spirits.

The most commonly talked about grief is the death of a loved one. In his book *Redeeming Heartache (2021)*, Dr. Dan B. Allender, describes the loss of a spouse, regardless of whether it is by death or divorce:

The widows I know want to talk. For them, the spouse who was lost is even more present than when he or she was alive. Memories pool under chairs and flow like a menacing river. Their appearance haunts and then fades just as quickly in a ghostlike haze. One widow I worked with said, "I remember his face so clearly that I can see the nicks from his shaving, and then he vanishes as if I'd never seen him before." Memories of a beloved are both comforting and cruel. A widow passes the living room that was once the intimate meeting place for conversation at the end of the day. She remembers the bottle of red wine being opened, a slab of cheese cut, and a few saltines adorning the plate. This time before dinner is hallowed, not to be profaned by television or a recitation of the current political morass. The particulars of the interaction might not be remembered by bedtime, but the sweetness lingers. Now the widow can barely skirt the room, let alone sit in the quilted chair and look at the empty seat where her husband once sat. What I have described about the way Becky and I leave the daytime hours behind has not yet been annihilated by death. We have not suffered losing each other through death or divorce. Yet, of all the terrors I know in life, this trauma is one that haunts me more than any other. As difficult as it was to write about being a stranger, and at times it was agonizing, imagining our life together torn from either of us feels like a trauma I can get only so close to before I go numb (p. vii).

The opening sentence of the book *A Grief Observed* by theological powerhouse C.S. Lewis is, *"No one ever told me that grief felt so like fear."* This book details Lewis' journey through grief after losing his beloved wife. Losing a spouse to death is one of the most intimate forms of loss. It is truly like losing a piece of yourself, which makes sense since Mark 10 tells us that marriage partners become one instead of two separate people. This all-encompassing grief is especially hard because there is no escape from it—our home, daily routine, vacation planning, and all the rituals we live in are inherently different when our spouse has passed away.

Whenever we experience the death of a loved one, specifically a spouse, we are left with a tough choice. We must decide whether to withdraw to protect ourselves from further loss or to open our hearts again and thrive. Which will we choose? That is the question for all of us who have lost a loved one.

The death of a child, whether through miscarriage, infant loss, child death, or the death of an adult child, is a heart-rending experience. The grief felt in these instances is perhaps worse because it flies in the face of what we believe should happen. Children expect to mourn their parents, not the other way around. It's often easier for parents to withdraw from their friends whose families are still whole than for them to put on a brave face at family functions or other events. This is true even if they still have living children. Parents who have lost a child often take out their anger on each other. This is a sad reality, but if they can get past it, they will find that they can be each other's biggest supporters because no one else really knows what they have lost.

I had a friend whose three-year-old daughter had cancer. In spite of the efforts to save her, she went home to be with the Lord. But in her three years on Earth, she did more than most people to lead people to Jesus. Prior to her illness, her parents were atheists. Grandparents and friends prayed for the family, and her parents accepted Jesus Christ as their Savior. The hundreds of people who were praying were significantly impacted. Their marriage stood the storm of loss and over time grew stronger and stronger, although it was a long, hard road through grief together.

Losing a parent at whatever age also causes extreme grief. While we know our parents will most likely not outlive us, we also find it difficult to imagine our lives without them. Parents are normally our most constant people—there from the day we were born. This makes the loss of them throw us into uncharted territory; we feel orphaned no matter how old we are. And for those of us with conflicted or distant relationships with our parents, the regret and pain that come with the final goodbye leave one feeling fragmented, perhaps with a sense of anger and frustration over unfinished business, which can be paralyzing.

There are so many other loved ones we might lose. The price of love is always, in this fallen world, that we will be forced to say goodbye at some point. Either they will leave this Earth, or we will. While we remain on Earth, we will be forced to walk the dark road of grief, but not alone, never alone.

But grief isn't limited to the loss of a loved one. There are other traumatic events or circumstances that can affect our lives, emotions, thinking, actions, and reactions as well.

The word for trauma in ancient Greek meant *"a wound or injury inflicted through an act of violence"* *(Allender, 2021, p. 237).*

Trauma is a complex topic that, until recently, was studied very little. It is a response to a terrible event such as an accident, natural disaster, or witnessing or being a victim of violence. (American Psychological

Association, 2021) Trauma responses can happen in your brain even if you are entirely uninjured physically. For this reason, the grief and fear accompanying trauma can be difficult for other people to understand. Sometimes trauma stems from an event that you are unwilling to talk about, such as rape or domestic violence. It can also be complicated with concurrent other losses. This is the case, for example, for a child who witnesses a school shooting and loses a good friend in that shooting. The trauma of witnessing an act of violence is compounded by the grief of a lost loved one.

Some first responders, while still suffering physically, mentally, and emotionally, continued to rush in to save those who couldn't save themselves. Then there are the troops who are fighting to defend our country and those in other countries. They have sacrificed to protect those who could not protect themselves. The families of the fallen soldiers grieve for the ones who paid the ultimate price with their lives. There are also the soldiers that have come home broken—often more than just physically.

The effects of trauma can be life-altering because trauma shapes and distorts your sense of self. Commonplace situations can begin to be intensely frightening. People who have experienced trauma may also experience physical symptoms like persistent headaches and nausea. If you have experienced a traumatic event, it's important to seek healing and help.

Some losses aren't as easily attributed to grief but are equally traumatic to our lives, and we need time to allow ourselves to grieve and forgive others and ourselves. We need God to come into these places in our hearts so that we don't allow the situation or circumstance to derail us from living well. God has a plan for us even during a crisis. We must allow Him into these parts of our lives as well.

I think divorce fits in this category because it affects more than just an individual or couple; it encompasses an entire family and their friends.

Divorce is the ripping apart of two halves of a whole. There is almost always grief involved for everyone concerned. This is true even when one person is abusive, and it's usually true even for the person who initiated the divorce. One of the problematic aspects of grieving in divorce is that you're grieving a relationship that has ended with a person who is still alive. This makes it different and more open-ended than grieving the death of a spouse, which can make processing your feelings and moving forward complicated. Your feelings towards your ex-spouse may be ambiguous; love mixed with anger or fear, sadness, relief, loneliness, and confusion are all common feelings in divorce.

In addition to the ambiguous grief you may be feeling, other components often go hand in hand with divorce and cause layers of grief. Loss of custody of children, even part-time, can compound feelings of loss. So can financial changes, leaving the home where your family has lived, and dealing with the grief and anger of your children. Often, because divorce implies wrongdoing, Christians experience guilt and shame during and after a divorce. To move forward, you must walk through all these emotions with God and allow Him to heal your heart.

Although perhaps less likely to be associated with the need to grieve, some events in our lives can consist of a small trauma or a significant life-changing trauma that we overlook when we think of grieving.

This can be a severe financial problem that causes an abrupt shift in how your life works, a loss of faith in God or a person, the loss of a job or career that has been important to you, or any other change that fundamentally alters your lifestyle. It can also include the significant life changes that happen when you retire or physical challenges that stop you from participating in activities that have been important in your life.

A friend of mine experienced this type of loss when her last child left home. She had immersed herself in being a mother for over twenty years: reading books, making sure school uniforms were ready, packing lunches, going to football and basketball games, and helping with homework and studying. She had a job, but the most important parts of her day were before and after work. When her youngest daughter left for college several states away, she would come home from work to a house that felt empty despite the continued presence of her husband. She didn't know how to spend all of the time she had spent on her children for so long. *"I knew it was good that they all moved out and had their own lives,"* she told me, "but that didn't stop me from tearing up in the cereal aisle of the grocery store because I didn't need to buy her favorite cereal anymore. We still talked often, but it wasn't the same as her being at home."

Despite her acknowledgment that this was how things were supposed to be, my friend still felt the grief of separation from her children. A loss of lifestyle might or might not be a bad thing, but losing your way of life is a loss. It often causes pain, even if it was expected or has positive elements.

The tragedy of addiction is that it has the power to derail your life as well as the lives of those around you. Few people walk into addiction purposely. For some, grief or trauma presents itself, and some substances provide relief. Others drink to be social, and somewhere in life, they go over the line into addiction without realizing it until it's too late. Looking back, they see a battlefield of wounded behind them. So their drinking continues. Eventually, they either experience a successful intervention, or their habit continues for the rest of their life.

It seems that relief tricks you into believing that this substance or activity is helpful when, in reality, it is harmful. By the time you realize the truth, addiction has kicked in. For others, such as myself, addiction starts with a social habit.

I began drinking when I was eighteen, just occasionally with friends. My use of alcohol escalated after my first marriage when I found myself in an abusive relationship. It helped to numb the pain of the blows. I went through a divorce but then realized that I was still drinking. Without my realizing it, alcohol had progressed from a coping mechanism to an addiction. When I was 24, I went to treatment. God used an inpatient treatment program, AA, and a counselor to keep me on track. I've been sober for 43 years now because of the voice of God and the accountability of those people and many others along the way.

My second husband, Marvin, had his first heart attack seven years after I started treatment. I remember sitting in front of the wood-burning stove and desperately wanting a drink. I had so much fear and pain, and I was sure that God and everyone else would understand if I just had a drink or two. I heard God's still, small voice tell me just to go to sleep instead and that I'd be alright in the morning. He was right. His voice reminded me—

not only was He watching, but all my AA friends were watching and supporting me, too. That accountability was one of the most powerful tools that God used in my recovery process. The beautiful thing is, that as I have stayed sober, He has used my life as a witness to those around me. They see that my faith in God has empowered me to have a rich, textured, sober life, one that is full and filled with joy even amid great pain and sorrow.

Although grieving is more associated with trauma, we live in a world full of tragedies. Whether we realize it or not, the whole world is a war zone. God will triumph in the end, but until that day, we live in a place where bad things happen around us every day. They don't have to affect us directly to cause grief; who can watch interviews with grieving parents after a school shooting or footage of the devastation of a war zone and remain unmoved? Tragedies don't just happen around us; they also happen to us. The phone that rings next with the news of an accident may be mine or yours.

Jesus spoke directly to tragedy in John 16, just before he endured his own tragedy—crucifixion. *"These things I have spoken to you so that in Me you may have peace. In the world you have tribulation, but take courage; I have overcome the world."* (John 16:33, NASB) The good news as we experience tragedy in our lives and in the world around us is that Jesus has overcome the world. We can take heart in that truth, even when our hearts are broken. There is hope in knowing we are sojourners here; this is not our final home. But while we are here, Jesus says we will have trouble. It is the nature of this world.

But then there are the things that slowly eat away at our world. Receiving the diagnosis of a debilitating disease, either for yourself or a loved one, is one of the hardest things you may have to face in life. Every new symptom or loss of ability is a new trauma. As the disease progresses, you are confronted with further losses.

Recently, I spoke with a friend at church who has been diagnosed with dementia. He told me how frustrated he often gets when he can't remember things because he knows why he can't remember them. Every forgetful moment reminds him of the disease he struggles with daily. He said the most challenging part is knowing that, barring a miracle, it will only get worse—it will never get better. I asked him how he continued to live in peace in that circumstance. His answer was phenomenal: "Every time I can remember something, I remember to thank God for it. And every time I can't remember, I remind myself that God is using even this."

Some tragedies produce grief, which is hard to talk about because they are outside of ordinary, socially acceptable events. People understand a lot of the traumas and tragedies that befall us, but a few are just hard to talk about with others. This can be because the cause of grief is one that you don't feel comfortable talking about or one that is not socially approved. It can also be that the scope of your grief response is more or less than what your culture deems normal.

One example of this might be a husband or child who dies by suicide. Often, a parent, spouse, or child may feel too grief-stricken to talk about it, and others may feel uncomfortable bringing it up. Any grief that you hesitate to talk about would fall in this category. People keep this kind of grief inside, refusing to talk about it out of guilt, shame, or a desire for it to just disappear. Unfortunately, grief that is held inside doesn't disappear; the only way out of grief is through.

A woman I know was pregnant with twins. She lost one but carried the other one to term, birthing a healthy baby boy. She talks about how she felt guilty for grieving her lost son, a feeling compounded by the people around her completely ignoring the fact that Noah had been a twin and focusing only on him. While this is understand-able—grief is uncomfortable and joy is not—it made her feel as though she couldn't express any sorrow for the child she lost. However, it was not until she was able to voice that grief that she began to work through it toward healing and restoration with God.

Other types of grief may be the loss of a dearly-loved pet, the death of an ex-spouse, or the loss of a co-worker or teacher. To others, these losses may seem more minor than they are, making you feel like you cannot express your grief.

I'm going to stop here for a moment to address the elephant in the room. What do I say to someone who is facing grief, and what do I not say? I was having dinner with a friend the other night. Both of us are widows and could talk about this sensitive topic. We discussed what not to say, keeping in mind that someone's journey may have been a long and hard illness, or multiple heart attacks, dementia, or alcoholism.

There were a few phrases that were spoken to my friend shortly after her husband died, which were not helpful, encouraging, or supportive. *"Isn't it a blessing he's gone?"* *"Well, you won't have to worry anymore."* *"You'll be fine; you're strong."* *"You can start a new chapter now without dealing with everything you've had to deal with."* *"Time heals."* *"You can start living."* *"It's a shame you wasted so much of your life."* *"How are you able to forgive him for all he's done?"* *"I bet now you sleep well."* Perhaps the people who said these words meant to be kind and supportive, but they didn't feel that way to her.

There were some supportive words and actions that helped me, as well as words that have been shared with me by others that helped them. *"I don't know what you are going through, but I want you to know I'm there for you, even if it's just to listen." "How can I help you?" "I will be praying for the peace of God to hold you close."*

The best words that anyone ever said to me were followed by actions that showed they meant them. *"I am here for you," and mean it. "I'll pray for you," and mean it. "I can listen, even if I don't have answers,"* and mean it. This kind of care is like water on parched land. Sometimes just giving someone a hug and a smile is just what they need.

It was always amazing after Steve passed that cards seemed to arrive at just the right time, every time. The meals left on my doorstep by my small group were wonderful! Every Friday at 6:00 a.m., my neighbor would come over and bring my garbage cans up to the street for pickup and back down at the end of the day. Every so often, his wife made pancakes for the family, and she would have him bring a serving over and put it on the front porch, then text me to let me know it was there. They didn't need to say anything to me; they just knew this is what they could do, and they did it without fanfare but with love. It is those things that let us know we are not alone. Those are the things that are cherished.

How Grief Can Affect Our Lives

We all know that grief is an emotional response. We expect that loss will wreak emotional havoc in our lives.

We expect that loss will cause emotions such as loneliness, sadness, anger, and guilt. But grief has much more far-reaching consequences than the expected emotional ones.

According to many experts, including Bessel van der Kolk, emotional stress triggers the same body systems as physical stress. Grief can also cause physical problems. Studies have shown that grief raises markers for inflammation throughout your body and suppresses your immune system. Grief can also be felt in your body in a tightness in your chest, nausea, food aversion, headaches, sensitivity to light, and tense muscles. Insomnia is common after loss, as is hypersomnia, both of which can lead to physical exhaustion. The stress response that grief sets off in your body can also temporarily elevate your blood pressure.

Physical symptoms of grief can be exacerbated if you refuse to deal with your feelings, choosing to avoid them rather than work through them. Living with unresolved grief for years can wreak havoc on your body. As painful as it can be to acknowledge the feelings and work through the grief you are experiencing, the alternative can be a life of poor health as your body is forced to live under the stress of unacknowledged grief. There is a book by Bessel van der Kolk called: *The Body Keeps Score: Brain, Mind, and Body in the Healing of Trauma.* My daughter gave it to me shortly after Steve passed away. It is a great book that opens the door to healing. It helps us heal not just current trauma but also events from our past that break down our bodies when they pile up inside us.

The spiritual significance of grief cannot be over-stated. So often, our grief prompts us to run from God instead of running toward Him. A major reason for this is that, often, when grief hits, we turn to idols to assuage our grief. We refuse to mourn, so we bury our grief and look for something to distract us.

For me, it was trying to fulfill my husband's legacy and not allowing myself to grieve. When he passed, I was busy trying to do what he asked of me instead of realizing that his legacy was his, not mine. As a result, I finally chose to intentionally grieve. In the process, I found God meeting me right there, and I remembered that my legacy is mine to choose. With God, we can grieve well; we can heal well.

God gives us grace and wisdom to fulfill our purpose in life and no one else's. Fulfilling our purpose takes intentionally pursuing an intimate relationship with God, the one who can heal even the deepest wounds in our hearts if we ask Him into those places. God is interested in our thriving, having peace that passes understanding, love that is unimaginable, and joy in all that we do, even when it is difficult.

It's easy to feel that vulnerability is the enemy when

your heart has broken. While self-protection can give you a sense of control, it's death to your spirit. Protecting your heart from feeling grief means you cannot allow yourself to feel a connection to anyone. This doesn't just set you up for emotional isolation; it sets you up for spiritual death. Control becomes your idol.

This desire to stay in control doesn't always look like spiritual death. I know of a family in which the husband was molested as a child. He never spoke about it—even his parents never knew what had happened. He never processed this traumatic experience and refused to feel any grief for what had happened to him. He stayed rigidly in control of his emotions, and even when he and his wife experienced the loss of a young child, he didn't express any sorrow. He was a pastor and spent his life pouring out for the people he ministered to in church. He appeared to be a model of a self-contained, unselfish family man with a strong faith in God. However, being in complete control came at a price—he was also completely unable to love his wife and children in a meaningful way. Keeping everyone at arm's length was his mechanism for staying in control. Eventually, as often happens when an idol takes God's place, his control failed him. He began to drink heavily in secret.

But the truth is, we aren't meant to be in control; God is. And when you try to lose your vulnerability, you end up losing so much more. Eventually, my friend's husband ended up hardening his heart to the point that he left the ministry, his family, and God. In trying to protect his heart, he ended up breaking it, along with so many others. The last time I spoke to him, he was full of regret, but his guilt was too strong to allow him to return to God and experience healing for the old pain, as well as the new pain he now faces.

Brain fog is another problem that often occurs when you are dealing with grief. This can take many forms. You may be unable to concentrate or have difficulty making even simple decisions. If you're experiencing the *"fog of grief,"* you may struggle to remember important tasks, lose things much more often than normal, and feel generally hazy.

This feeling of mental unreality or fogginess can feel frustrating, but it's your body's defense mechanism to help the loss sink in gradually. It may pass quickly, or it may come and go for some time. Either way, give yourself grace—it's difficult to process grief, and your brain is doing its best.

The relational fallout from grief can be severe.

One of the biggest problems grief causes is isolation. Often, when we are experiencing grief, we pull away from people, feeling that they don't understand. And they may also distance themselves simply because grief makes people uncomfortable. Isolation can come in the form of actual aloneness, a decision to stay away from others. This can make you feel as though you're protecting your heart; it can also be painful to return to the normal rhythms of life when you're still mourning. But isolation can also be felt in a room full of people, as grief produces a sense of solitariness internally. It's as if grief tries to tell you that you are the only one who understands, as though no one else has experienced this type of pain before.

The reality I have found is that people are there for those who are mourning for thirty days and then go back to their own lives. Then the quiet sets in. That is when we need to intentionally choose to connect with others. A friend of mine, when her husband of fifty years passed away after a long, slow rehab from an accident, felt overwhelmed by people checking in on her. As the phone rang and rang, she just wanted to be left alone. I told her that she should take the calls while they were coming because soon the phone would stop ringing. It did. She was amazed; she was sure life would, in a sense, continue as it was. I think the hardest part was realizing that her new normal would be drastically different from her old one. Faith and family are the keys for her to keep moving forward.

Isolation can be dangerous emotionally for anyone who grieves. The truth is that God has designed us to work through pain together. Grief often brings guilt and shame with it. At the end of anything, whether it's a relationship, a job, or the life of a loved one, there is always someplace that we can look back at and doubt our choices. And this guilt-fueled regret can drive us to isolate ourselves further because if we let anyone get too close to our pain, we are afraid they will also see what we should have done differently and pass judgment. So we bury our regrets in isolation, but the damage this does to our hearts is immense. To successfully bury your regret, your heart will need to be isolated and hardened enough to keep those who love you away. This is usually accomplished by treating people with contempt and refusing to care for their needs. This isn't only bad for those around you; it's bad for you too.

The consequences of isolation can be even more far-reaching for a person who must make major decisions in the midst of grief. The brain fog that is common during grieving can cloud your decision-making faculties, leaving space for lapses in judgment. So for those who are forced to make possibly life-changing choices during this time without receiving help from someone who cares for them and is in a less foggy place, the consequences can be disastrous. For this reason, as well as your emotional health, it's essential to avoid isolation while grieving. Accept help from those who love you and have your best interests at heart!

In addition to isolation, grief often causes conflict between grieving people. Whether it's because each one believes the other one doesn't care enough or cares too much or because the anger and regret that grief often brings with it turns outward and flows onto the people you love most, grief is a bringer of conflict. When we are in pain, it's easy to lash out at everyone around us, even when they're trying to help. This can lead to serious conflict over even small details and relationship-ending fights that can actually exacerbate grief between people who are already grieving.

There Is Hope

As we've gone through the components of grief, where it comes from, and all of the ways it can affect us, it's easy to feel that grief will devastate your life. But there is hope! God promised in His word that He would be with us. Psalm 34:18 says, *"The Lord is near to the broken-hearted and saves the crushed in spirit"* (ESV), and Jesus repeated the promise in the Beatitudes when He said, *"Blessed are those who mourn, for they shall be comforted"* (Matt. 5:4 ESV).

The promises of comfort and the closeness of God are promises that we can cling to on the hardest days. Because He is faithful to His promises, we can rest assured that He will comfort us, put our hearts back together, and use the very circumstances of our grief to further His good plan in our lives.

Reflection

- What are some of the ways you have experienced the effects of grief in your life?

- In what way can you surrender control of your circumstances to God today?

2

WHEN GOD SAYS NO

"I sat in my prayer closet, screaming at God internally.
All those promises, all the times you've done miracles,
and now... nothing?
And I heard Jesus say to my heart, 'Even I received a no
from the Father in Gethsemane."

This is an excerpt of a journal entry that was written by a friend of mine just after the death of her child. It's a reminder that even Jesus, in His humanity, asked for something that He didn't get. And His response to that can guide us in our response when we also receive a no from the Father.

God Cares for Us

When we are grieving, we hear it all the time, but it's easy to forget the reality that God cares about the pain we are experiencing and the heartbreak we have. But David wrote in Psalm 56, *"You keep track of all my sorrows. You have collected all my tears in your bottle. You have recorded each one in your book"* (v. 8, ESV).

God does care, even when He doesn't do the thing we hoped He would do. This has to be the foundation of our response to God's denial of our requests. His refusal is anchored in His all-knowing goodness—His ability to see what will be best for His plan for us. If we can be secure in this knowledge, it becomes easier—although still not easy—to accept the no with which He answered while continuing to believe in His love and care for us.

Think about the context of a God who suffers with us even when He has the means to change the outcome to alleviate our suffering. If we believe in the sovereignty of God, we have to face this truth—He could take away the cause of our suffering. Instead, He asks us to suffer. He knows that the suffering will reap a reward both in us and in those around us. So, He asks us to do it, but He doesn't stop there. He goes through the suffering with us. We are asked to suffer sometimes, but we are never asked to suffer alone.

We sometimes hear about God caring for us in a way

that can make us disenchanted with Him when we experience trouble. We expect that because God hears and cares, He will say yes. Certainly, we expect Him to act when our suffering or the suffering of those we love is on the line.

But Hebrews 5 tells a different story, *"During the days of Jesus' life on earth, he offered up prayers and petitions with fervent cries and tears to the one who could save him from death, and he was heard because of his reverent submission. Son though he was, he learned obedience from what he suffered and, once made perfect, he became the source of eternal salvation for all who obey him"* (v. 7–9, NIV). So, Jesus—the perfect Son, God incarnate—experienced the same thing. He asked, in tears, to be spared from the cross. He pleaded with His Father for a different way. And the verse assures us that God heard Him. Yet, Jesus went to the cross. He obeyed even in His grief—and in that obedience, He not only attained salvation for all of us but also showed us how to respond when God says no.

In Matthew 26, we see Jesus pleading for relief. He told His disciples that His soul was *"overwhelmed with sorrow to the point of death"* (v. 38, NIV). He then prayed this prayer, *"My Father, if it is possible, may this cup be taken from me. Yet not as I will, but as you will"* (v. 39, NIV). Luke 22:44 tells us that Jesus was in such anguish that His sweat became like drops of blood. This rare physical phenomenon called hematohidrosis can occur in great mental, emotional, or physical crises (Jaju et al., 2009). Jesus suffered greatly, and He asked God to take His pain away if it was possible. But God said no. And after asking three times to be released from the anguish of dying on the cross and temporary separation from His Father, we see in verse 46 that Jesus goes to meet Judas and the soldiers who are coming to arrest Him. This is the ultimate example of surrendering to the will of God.

God Protects Us

This is so difficult for us to say when we are grieving. Over and over, the Bible speaks of God's protection over His people. It tells us that God will intervene on our behalf. When we experience suffering, these verses seem to mock us. We have no choice if we are going to continue to trust and believe God, but to reconcile those verses—which we know to be true—with our reality, even when our reality seems to contradict them. If God's Word does not seem true to me, it's not a sign that His Word is wrong. It's a sign that there's a foundational truth I don't understand yet, and I need to uncover it and let its truth work in me.

Uncovering this truth in the Bible isn't difficult if we are looking for it, but it often goes overlooked. This is not because it's hard to see, but because we would rather not see it. In multiple passages in the Gospels, Jesus prepares His disciples to face grief, persecution, and suffering. One notable example comes from Matthew 10:

I am sending you out like sheep among wolves. Therefore be as shrewd as snakes and as innocent as doves. Be on your guard; you will be handed over to the local councils and be flogged in the synagogues. On my account, you will be brought before governors and kings as witnesses to them and to the Gentiles. But when they arrest you, do not worry about what to say or how to say it. At that time you will be given what to say, for it will not be you speaking, but the Spirit of your Father speaking through you.

Brother will betray brother to death, and a father his child; children will rebel against their parents and have them put to death. You will be hated by everyone because of me, but the one who stands firm to the end will be saved. When you are persecuted in one place, flee to another. Truly I tell you, you will not finish going through the towns of Israel before the Son of Man comes.

The student is not above the teacher, nor a servant above his master. It is enough for students to be like their teachers, and servants like their masters. If the head of the house has been called Beelzebul, how much more the members of his household! (v. 16–25, NIV)

Jesus prepared them to be imprisoned, betrayed,

beaten, and even killed. This was only a few verses after he had given them extraordinary power—the power to heal, cast out demons, and proclaim the Gospel. Looking at it from our perspective, it doesn't sound like they would be protected at all! He let them know up front that the job He was asking them to do would be dangerous and that they might lose their lives. And He seemed to be okay with that. But in that case, how are we protected?

Reading on in the same passage, we encounter these words, *"Do not be afraid of those who kill the body but cannot kill the soul. Rather, be afraid of the One who can destroy both soul and body in hell"* (v. 28, NIV). Here's our first clue—His protection doesn't offer a free pass on suffering in this world, just in the next one.

But just in case we think that God doesn't care about our suffering or even our lives, He continued in the next verse with these words, *"Are not two sparrows sold for a penny? Yet not one of them will fall to the ground outside your Father's care. And even the very hairs of your head are all numbered. So don't be afraid; you are worth more than many sparrows"* (v. 29–31, NIV). So, God's priority is the advancement of the Kingdom of God, yet He cares deeply about us and our suffering. His priorities are just different from ours—His priorities are eternal instead of earthly.

Until our priorities align with His—until we care more about our souls than our bodies—we won't understand why some of our prayers seem to go unanswered. John recorded the prayer that Jesus prayed for protection for His disciples, both the ones who had walked physically with Him and those who would come later, including us. It's a beautiful prayer, full of powerful words of protection and safety. *"My prayer is not that you take them out of the world but that you protect them from the evil one" (v.* 15, NIV). *"I have given them the glory that you gave me, that they may be one as we are one"* (v. 22, NIV). But towards the end, we see what He is asking for protection for when He says, *"Father, I want those you have given me to be with me where I am, and to see my glory, the glory you have given me because you loved me before the creation of the world"* (v. 24, NIV). He is asking for protection for our souls. He wants us to be where He is for eternity. This is the protection Jesus sought for us—eternal protection from the evil one, who would like to claim our souls for his own. Author Nancy Guthrie writes:

When I open my eyes to see Jesus on the cross, I can no longer harbor resentment that he hasn't come through for me in the ways I have wanted him to—ways that are so limited by my earthly perspective. I can no longer insist that his promises of protection apply to everything that threatens my comfortable existence in this life. (p. 68)

Satan will use our grief to separate us from God if we

let him. There are a few ways he will try to make us believe that God neither cares for us nor protects us. Anger, fear, and disappointment are three common emotions that grief sparks inside us. If we let him, Satan will manipulate these normal emotions to try to turn us away from God.

Don't Succumb to Anger

When I was 39, I lost a husband to heart disease. He had nine heart attacks in six years. Marvin was a happy soul for most of our marriage, but he became angry in his grief after about the seventh heart attack. His anger was directed at everything and everyone.

One morning, I walked into the room where he was sitting. I said, *"We get that you're angry about the toll the heart attacks have taken on you. But the legacy you leave is your choice. I can't choose it for you; only you can determine that. We get that one day; you will die. But you can either leave us with memories of your nuggets of wisdom that we can use in our lives when you're gone, or you can leave us with memories of your anger. The choice is yours. What will your legacy be?"*

The grief was real, but there was the God factor. Marvin decided he wanted a different legacy than anger.

He had sown God's love, grace, and joy into the lives of hundreds of people who struggled with addiction. He did that for his family, too. He was a man who loved God and those whom God put in his path. That is the legacy he chose. He brought God into the middle of his grief. His funeral was a testament to that.

The grief was real for me, too. I also had choices to make. I left for a speaking engagement, where I talked to a group of chronic caregivers right after that confrontation. A little voice inside me said, *"So, what will your legacy be?"* That question hit me hard—just because I wasn't in the same position as Marvin physically didn't mean I shouldn't think about my legacy. That question has been my proverbial plumb line ever since. Did I want to be known for how I worked a lot or for being a great mother, daughter, or Granny? Those were good, but I didn't want them to be my legacy. I wanted my legacy to be that I knew God and His love and that those who saw me could see His love for them in me.

Don't Give In to Fear

In John 16:33, Jesus tells us, *"I have told you these things, so that in Me you may have peace. In this world you will have trouble. But take heart! I have overcome the world"* (NIV). It's easier to do this some days than on other days when you're in the midst of trouble. But this I know—His peace is more significant than anything we could imagine. Peace is the opposite of fear. How wonderful it is that Jesus offers peace even in the middle of difficulties!

It is a choice to keep our minds steadfast and to trust Him. It doesn't always come easily, but that choice is the path to peace. Psalm 23 gives us this example, *"Even though I walk through the valley of the shadow of death, I will fear no evil, for you are with me; your rod and your staff, they comfort me"* (v. 4, ESV).

We sometimes have to ask the Holy Spirit, who lives in us, to give us the strength to trust Him when we need it. God wants us to have peace in our souls, and He has given us the pathway to gain peace amid trouble. When we know He is in control and that He has our best interests in mind, it becomes easier to trust His plan. Trust is the path away from fear—not trusting that God will do what we want Him to do, but trusting that He will do what He knows is best in light of eternity.

Don't Allow Disappointment to Take Root

If we don't allow the Holy Spirit to rewrite our priorities, aligning them with God's priorities, we will live in disappointment with God. We won't understand why He answers some prayers and not others. It will feel capricious and cruel. Once we have allowed Him to do that work in us, however, we may still face disappointment. There may be times when we don't see how a particular event could further the Kingdom of God. We may still not understand how God could let something happen—tragedies that seem senseless and life-shattering.

When we feel disappointed in God's answer, we have to lean on our trust in Him. Disappointment that is allowed to take root will turn into bitterness, making us feel like our lives are over because of this loss or pain. If left unchecked, bitterness can lead to rebellion against the only One who can take our pain away.

As counter-intuitive as it seems, the antidote to disappointment is gratitude. It can be immensely difficult to be grateful while experiencing grief. Yet, it's the way back out of the black hole of bitterness that prolonged disappointment with God brings. Intentionally being grateful as a part of your grieving process puts you back on the path to joy. Gratitude helps you recover from grief, while disappointment only prolongs your suffering. Long ago, I read a quote, the source of which is disputed, that said, *"How lucky I am to have something which makes saying goodbye so hard"* (Goodreads Librarian Group, 2015). What a beautiful frame for grief: This loss is harder because of the beauty that preceded it—so I will be grateful for the beauty even as I mourn the loss.

When we turn our hearts toward God, the Holy Spirit can work in us and change our disappointment with God, others, and ourselves into gratitude. Gratitude that His plan will lead us to exactly where He wants us to go, gratitude for the people around us even when they hurt us, and gratitude that God cares for me and is working in me even when I have wrought destruction in my own life. Learning to feel and express gratitude, even in grief, is a process, so you need to commit to the practice, especially if you find yourself struggling with ongoing disappointment. Begin to name the things that you are most grateful for, thanking God for each one. Remembering in this way can help you move forward in your grief to a place where you are not only expressing gratitude for having had what you've now lost, but also for what you currently have.

God Walks With Us

They say there are at least five stages of grief: denial, anger, bargaining, depression, and acceptance. When we allow God to walk with us in our grief, I have found that the stages are still there; however, we are not alone as we go through them. These stages don't happen in a neat, tidy time frame; they aren't predictable. Each of us grieves differently, and God walks the dark road of grief with each of us. *"When you pass through the waters, I will be with you; and when you pass through the rivers, they will not sweep over you. When you walk through the fire, you will not be burned; the flames will not set you ablaze"* (Isaiah 43:2, NIV).

He doesn't promise that we won't walk through rivers or fires, even though we wish that's what He said. He does promise, however, to be with us the whole time we are there—no matter how many times you have to walk through the same river or the same fire, no matter how long you stay angry, no matter how many times you try to bargain with Him. He's not going anywhere. He will be right there with you. And I know that when God is brought into the middle of the pain, He provides a way to heal and to reach out to comfort others and find comfort in return. He brings peace to the most challenging places—where guilt, shame, pain, and loss melt in the presence of His grace and love.

Whether it's the loss of a person, a job or lifestyle, a home, a marriage, or any of the other losses that fill us with grief, every loss has this in common: we grieve for the past. We look backward and wish that we could go back to a time before—before that death; before I made the mistake that got me fired; before I got sick. We also grieve for the future. We cannot—and don't want to—imagine a future without those things or people. But hear God tell you that He will be with you as you move into the future.

Shortly after my husband Marvin's death, another widow came up to me and prayed this over me, *"God, show her that there is life after death."* Then she told me, *"If you ever forget that, call me. I will remind you that you have a life, purpose, and plan even after your husband's death."* God wasn't finished with His plan for my life, and He isn't finished with His plan for your life either.

When God says no to our requests, when He allows trouble and loss to come into our lives, we get to choose to allow Him to walk with us, protecting and caring for us as we grieve. The testimony of God's grace and love that we will have as we allow Him to work in our hearts will not only change us, it will change those around us. As I mentioned in the last chapter, when Marvin had his first heart attack, and I was tempted to drink just a little bit to cope, God's presence helped me to stay sober. At a meeting a few months later, a younger AA member came up to me at a meeting and said, *"I figured if you couldn't stay sober with your faith, there was no hope for me. But you stayed sober! I need to have that same faith, so tell me how."* God used my life to advance His Kingdom, even in the midst of my pain. And He can do the same with your life, wherever you are, if you allow Him to be present in the middle of your grief and to walk through it with you.

Reflection

- What is one way God has shown His care for you in your suffering?

- In what area of your heart do you need to replace your anger, fear, or disappointment with God with grace-fueled gratitude?

- What step can you make in that direction today?

3

FINDING SUPPORT WHILE GRIEVING

"Acceptance is not about liking a situation. It is about acknowledging all that has been lost and learning to live with that loss."

—Elisabeth Kubler-Ross and David Kessler

A s we grieve, we are forced to accept that life will move forward without the person or thing we have lost. We must find normalcy in the new routines, places, and people around us. We live in a culture that obsessively pushes people to get over grief, return to normal, and make it out of the other side, as though grief is only a tunnel through to an unchanged landscape. Those who have experienced grief know that this isn't the case. There is no normal to return to for us.

'Normal' life intrudes on our grief when we have to pay bills, grocery shop, or give the children a bath. But it isn't normal—life is different because we are different. Often, the phrase *"new normal"* makes our skin crawl. We don't want this to be our new normal. We would like to resist this new normal, which is why we continue fighting against our grief. But the way forward is to go through the grief—there is no way around it. I have found that it's much easier to go through grief with support. God is always with us and will provide support for us to lean on in our grief.

This support often comes in the form of other people who have suffered or are suffering in similar ways. I believe this is what 2 Corinthians 1 means when it says, *"Praise be to the God and Father of our Lord Jesus Christ, the Father of compassion and the God of all comfort, who comforts us in all our troubles so that we can comfort those in any trouble with the comfort we ourselves have received from God"* (v. 3–4, NIV). We receive comfort and turn around and give it to someone else, who in turn gives back to us the comfort they have received from God. In this way, God uses us in our grief to comfort each other.

The Support of Friends and Family

Family Support

Most of us have the support of our families, although not all of us. We have someone that we can call—someone who also feels our loss. Since Steve passed, one of the many family members who have supported me is my sister-in-law. She and I have grown closer than we were when he was alive. We joke that either of us can call the other for a ten-minute yell when we need to just get something off our chest.

Sometimes we have family members who want to support us, to be there for us. They just don't know how. Because we each grieve differently, they don't know if remembering the funny story about our lost loved one will make us feel better or worse. They're not sure if we want to talk about the loss of whatever we are grieving, need help making plans for moving forward, or just want someone to sit in silence with us. Because our families know us better than anyone else, we often expect them to just figure it out. Then when they don't, it's easy to feel hurt and angry because we are already hurting inside.

Let your family know how they can support you.
Would it bring healing to you to have someone help with
daily life necessities for a little while until your brain
feels clearer? Ask them for that. Do you need a meal
every week after you go for treatment? Ask for that.
Maybe you called your mom on Saturday morning every
week for twenty years, and now Saturday mornings are
filled with sadness for you. Find out if your aunt wants a
phone call every Saturday; maybe it will help both
of you.

It might be that your family won't step up to the plate
if given the chance to support you. If that's the case,
don't worry. Find a local church or group of close friends
that can support and encourage you while you're
grieving.

Part of my healing was accomplished by creating
new memories with my grandkids. This is a way to
remember the past and build new experiences for healing. One such memory-building experience was being a
part of Feeding the Five Thousand, an episode of The
Chosen. The Chosen is a series about Jesus, His life, and
the apostles.

The grandkids wanted Steve and me to watch the
series with them so we could share that memory. Every
time they came, we watched it again. After Steve passed,
it fell to the wayside in our home because there was an

empty chair. They continued to follow the series in their own home, and one day I heard from their mom there was a chance to be part of the filming of the episode of Feeding the Five Thousand. It was a long shot, but I applied.

The news came the day before Christmas that we got to go. I printed the acceptance email, put it in a Christmas card, and gave it to my grandson, Christian, as one of his Christmas presents. Christian was the most avid lover of The Chosen. When he opened it, he burst into tears and buried his head on the couch, crying. I asked what was wrong. He said nothing was wrong; it was just the best Christmas present he had ever received.

Filming was on June 8, 2022, in Texas. It was 108°F with high humidity, but we were in heaven. The kids talked about Grandpa a bit, but the memory of going with Grandma, no matter the obstacles, was the memory they had. I asked Christian when we were on the bus to the hotel if he had thought we would get to come. He shook his head. He hadn't believed that it would be possible with the obstacles we faced, but we agreed then and there that the memories were priceless and that it was all worth it. It was healing for all of us to have the time to remember something that both Steve and I did with the kids while building new memories that brought peace and joy to our hearts.

Supporting (And Being Supported By) Your Children

After Steve passed away, I found that my children were also grieving. Sometimes, we are so caught up in our grief that we forget that our children, whether still young or adults, are also mourning when a member of the family passes away or is diagnosed with a terminal illness. They mourn their relationship with that person. In my case, my children were grieving for a man who had been their father figure for a long time. They loved and respected Steve and were grieving as much as I was, just in a different way. They needed my support as much as I needed theirs.

My grandkids also needed to be allowed to grieve. Although the relationship was different, Grandpa was also a part of their lives. I need to continue to help them through their grief, even if sometimes it's only listening, hugging, holding, praying for, and acknowledging their loss and sadness.

One of my grandsons recently found an old iPhone that Grandpa had given him years ago. Although the pictures that were on it were from years past, he loved going through those memories of his grandfather, by himself or with his family. Unselfishly, he gave me the iPhone. He wanted to make me happy, and help me with my grief. It was a hard gift for him because he cherished the memories that were on that phone. I loved the gift, and it made me happy to look at the pictures. It also made me happy that he cared enough about me and my pain to give it to me. However, when his mom told me the price of that gift for him, I decided I wanted to appreciate his gift, but allow him to keep it so that he would have the memories. Often, it is easier to think of our grief than to remember that others are also grieving, but that isn't God's plan for us.

I didn't do as well with remembering to support my children in their grief when Marvin passed. I was only 39 then, and the death of my husband rocked my world. Our adopted grandma was there for the kids to support them in their grief. I wish I had known then what I know today so that I could have been better support for them in the midst of their grief.

Many children also want to be a support for their grieving parent, similar to my grandson wanting to give me the iPhone. I had a friend whose husband passed away when her daughter was fourteen. This teenage girl, who was grieving the loss of her father, found a trusted adult to take her to the store and help her bake her mom a birthday cake while her mom was at work, a job she and her dad had done together since she was young. She surprised her mom with it on the evening of her birthday. Even though it didn't make the pain of her loss go away, my friend said that cake was like a balm for her soul. And, as is often the case, it was healing for her daughter, too. Remember the verse in 2 Corinthians? We are comforted when we bring comfort to others.

Close Friends

Even if we can count the number of close friends we have on one hand, we are blessed to have them regardless. These are the people that, no matter what, are there for you. These are the people who, when they wake up in the middle of the night thinking about you, pray, assuming God put you on their hearts for a reason.

Mark and Joanna are two such friends for me. These are friends who stayed an extra week to be near me and help with a funeral during the COVID-19 pandemic. They are friends who would drive twenty-one hours to be there for you without notice. They are friends that I consider closer than family. When I'm in a painful place, they know and understand.

Everyone needs a few friends like this—a group you

can trust with your emotions, heart, decisions (both good and bad), highs, and lows. They can be trusted to share their insight, experience, and hope no matter what. Sometimes they don't need to say a thing other than *"I love you."* The people who fill this role for us are treasured gifts from God. We need to treat them as such and never take them for granted.

The Support of a Counselor or Spiritual Leader

Counselors

When I was in AA, I came through a secular treatment program with an agnostic counselor. I was from a conservative Catholic home, and I got saved two years before I ended up in treatment.

God used my first counselor to help me to learn to forgive myself. He had me write on a blackboard how I thought I prioritized things in my life. I gave him my list in this order:

1. God
2. Myself

3. My daughter

4. My work

"Not true," he replied.

I countered with a heated, *"Yes it is!"*

"You need to put your name above God because you say you are a Christian and that you believe that God sent His son for the forgiveness of your sins, but you require more of yourself for your sins than He does. By not forgiving yourself, you are saying you were hurt more than God, and you would require more than God requires for the forgiveness of yourself and others. So until you are willing to forgive yourself and others, put your name above God." This statement was a powerful reminder for me that when God says I am forgiven, I am forgiven.

Years later, after long stints in China and while dealing with some business problems, Steve began going to a counselor, Kevin. A few years after Steve began talking to Kevin, I decided that I needed to start seeing him too. I was struggling to deal with the death of my father, the changes that Steve's business struggles meant for our lives and my grief over the difference between the life I'd dreamed of for us and our reality.

Kevin helped Steve and me develop tools for dealing with trauma and disappointments, and these tools have served me well for the rest of my life. Kevin helped Steve and me when we were dealing with his father's death and helped me through the grief and major decisions I had to make after Steve lost his battle with cancer.

We sometimes feel like needing to go to a counselor means that we are weak or not good enough Christians. Nothing could be further from the truth. Some grief, trauma, tragedies, and stressors need to be handled with a professional. Jesus calls us into healing, and when we have experienced something that we need tools to handle, a counselor can give us those tools. We can use them to maximize our strengths and to seek the healing Jesus calls us toward. When grief is too much for us, there is nothing stronger or more Godly than seeking help to deal with it.

Spiritual Leaders

A spiritual leader—whether that's a pastor, a small group leader, or another minister that you respect—can also provide helpful insight and tools to process grief. The wonderful thing about having both a counselor and a pastor that you can talk to is that they have different toolboxes that they can use to give you tools. A counselor looks at situations through the eyes of a professional; a good pastor or spiritual leader looks at them through the eyes of the Spirit. Both of these can be helpful when you're grieving.

Spiritual leaders have studied the Scriptures to help the people in their congregations see their problems from a Biblical perspective. They can help you look for God's faithfulness even in hard times. As an added benefit, spiritual leaders are usually highly invested in caring for and praying for the people God has given them to shepherd.

Finding a Supportive Community

Prayer Partners

These people become a small, trusted group that you can send a message to when you're struggling. I have a group of people who do this for me—I can just say, *"Need your prayers, friend,"* and they pray with fierce determination on my behalf.

During a severe upheaval in my business, I remember telling a friend, *"I'm sitting here in the Chick-fil-A parking lot having an ice cream cone and listening to Andrea Bocelli... It's not working!"* (Usually, when I'm in a stressful place, that helps.) As the words came out of my mouth, it occurred to me that I hadn't reached out to my group of prayer partners. So I stopped and sent my traditional text to the group. It didn't change the circumstances or my stress levels but it did change my perspective on the challenge. Once I was reminded that I have the freedom to choose my response even if I can't change the circumstances, I was free.

I know that when you are willing to reach out to God, He answers. He may not answer by changing the circumstances, but He will certainly empower you in the situation with wisdom, strength, and peace—an incredible peace deep within. Reaching out to others to pray with and for you is essential to finding the support you need when dealing with grief.

Small Groups

Many churches have small groups that are a part of their discipleship programs. If your church has such a program, I highly encourage you to be a part of a group. Small groups can be a wonderful source of support when you're grieving, and they give you an outlet to comfort others as you are comforted.

Our small group was extraordinary during Steve's illness. They prayed for us, brought meals and cards, and

brought my husband to medical appointments and proce-
dures. After Steve passed away, they extended me the
opportunity to stay with the group, even though it was a
couples' group. I was the first widow the group had the
opportunity to help in this way. The stability that came
from being with the group was incredible.

Over the past two years, I have been allowed to
grieve and grow, knowing there was a group committed
to my stability in faith, family, and business. They have
said I bring much to the group. Maybe this is true, but I
have received more than I could have ever anticipated.

The opportunity to be a part of a small group that has
walked with me through my pain has felt as though God
was holding me close to His heart and letting me know
He was always nearby. They have taught me how to
reach out again, both to give help and to receive it. I will
forever be grateful for their love and care for me.

Learning to Support Our Own Healing

This section will be full of practical tips to help you take
care of yourself physically while you deal with grief.
This might not seem very spiritual to you, but our spirits
live inside of the bodies God has given us. Taking care of
yourself is a Godly way to support yourself through your
grief.

Sleep

Grief is puzzling. It makes you so tired that everything seems too difficult, yet it keeps you awake with your mind buzzing. Learning to quiet the thoughts that keep you awake can be difficult, but there are some practical ways to help yourself sleep better. Getting between seven and eight hours of sleep a night can help your brain be clearer during the day when you need to be able to think, plan, or process your emotions. Ideally, going to bed by 10 p.m. will give you the best chance of achieving this goal. Limit your caffeine in the afternoon. Instead of watching television in the evening, read a good book or listen to relaxing music. Try not to eat large meals late in the evening, as this can keep your body awake longer. Avoid sleeping during the day since this will make it much harder to sleep at night. Try to be outside for at least 20 minutes a day; or if that's not possible, keep your blinds and curtains open during the day to let sunlight in. Sunlight is helpful for setting your body's sleep rhythms.

In the evening, pray and meditate on Scripture to help your mind relax. You might want to do some stretching or yoga to help your body relax as well. When you go to bed, a sound machine or softly playing instrumental music can help you fall asleep. Turning off the lights is helpful for getting your body to fall into a deeper sleep.

Nutrition

Have you ever noticed that things seem worse when you haven't eaten? That's because our bodies have built-in systems that need calories and water to function properly. When we don't eat or we binge on too much food, we activate the same symptoms and our blood sugar either plummets or skyrockets. This impact causes us to be moodier, easily frustrated, or makes us feel fatigued.

Grieving doesn't need to mean that we don't take care of our body's nutritional needs. Making a decision to eat something healthy even when you don't want to or to drink water instead of soda can have a big impact on how well you handle your grief and treat those around you.

Though I am not an expert in this area, what I know is that when I choose to make a different choice in what I eat or choose to be more intentional with my hydration, I am making the choice to be better and healthier for myself. I know my ability to heal depends on my ability to give myself grace in this area.

Exercise

Exercising can be extremely helpful during grief. There are many reasons for that. The first is that exercise naturally releases endorphins. These hormones create good feelings inside of you. The effect of endorphins when you're grieving can be to just take the edge off of your emotions.

Another struggle that exercise can help with is appetite. Often, one of the effects of grief is that you just aren't hungry. Supplying your body with nutrients can be difficult when you have no appetite. Exercise, even just walking for fifteen to twenty minutes out in the sunshine, can whet your appetite and help you want to put something nutritious in your body.

One other helpful aspect of exercise is that it can help your body tire during the day, allowing you to sleep better. Better sleep is paramount to our physical well-being, and exercising during the day is a great way to encourage your body to sleep during the night.

Maybe you have some close friends that you could walk with at a park near you, or perhaps you could swim at a nearby pool or take an exercise class at a local gym. These simple actions can help you in so many different ways, from endorphins to better sleep to connections with other people.

Kindness

Grief can sometimes make us unkind to ourselves. We want to handle loss *"better"* than we are handling it. This can cause us to mentally berate ourselves, tell ourselves to toughen up, or feel ashamed of our own perceived weaknesses. Remind yourself to be kind to yourself. This grief you are facing—this storm that has wrecked the life you had before—does not have a prescribed path. Ask God to help you to give yourself the same grace He gives you, then lean into the grace He provides.

Kindness towards others can help us heal, too. There is a project called the Kindness Project, started by Dr. Joan Cacciatore for parents who have lost children. Participants do random acts of kindness and service for others, usually complete strangers. They leave a card that honors their lost loved one by name. Whether you decide to look for this group online and join them in their endeavor or use the idea in your own way, the act of blessing others in our grief can be extremely healing. While suffering on the cross, Jesus took the time to reassure the thief who expressed belief, *"Truly I tell you, today you will be with me in paradise"* (Luke 23:43, NIV). We too can follow His example in this when we are suffering.

Reflection

- Who has God given you for support during your grieving, and how can you be a blessing to them?

- How can you support your own healing by taking care of yourself in the areas of sleep, nutrition, exercise, and kindness?

- What is one practical step you could take toward that today?

4

NAVIGATING GRIEF

Before there was GPS, there were navigators. A navigator's job was to plan the route and avoid the various hazards along the way. There is an interesting story about the Titanic, arguably the most famous shipwreck in history. According to the company's records, the navigator was removed from the ship's roster just a few days before it sailed. He was transferred to another ship, one that the company deemed needed his services more. Since they didn't have time to replace him, the Titanic sailed without a navigator. We all know how that went! Grief is a route filled with potential disasters, so it's important to listen to our Navigator—the Holy Spirit.

Having experienced suffering, we can turn around and help others who are behind us on the journey. One of the most redemptive parts of having experienced trauma or loss is the ability to help others navigate similar loss. Grief must be endured, even embraced, for us to navigate our way through it.

Celebrate the Good

Celebration of Life

Having a celebration of life ceremony after the death of a loved one rather than focusing on only the loss is one way to embrace grief and work toward healing. What are some things that your loved one enjoyed, and how can you celebrate them and their love? Maybe you can have people write out memories or record them on video. Perhaps celebrating their favorite music or giving seedlings so that people can plant a tree in their honor seems like a good fit. Whatever you think would bring a smile to their face can be a celebration of their life and can help those grieving to mourn.

A celebration of life ceremony has more flexibility than a traditional funeral. It can include traditional elements like readings and hymns, but it doesn't have to. You can include non-traditional elements such as floating lanterns, a fireworks display, or a concert by their favorite local band. Hosting a celebration of your loved one's life gives you the freedom to create an event that captures the essence of who they were and celebrates them in a personal way.

Even after the time for a celebration of life ceremony has passed, celebrating the person you've lost can help you work through your grief. About four months after Steve passed away, Robby (my grandson, who was 15 at the time with a permit to drive) called me and asked if I wanted to go get an ice cream cone together. I said I would, so I picked him up, and then he drove. I didn't realize what he was doing until he put on Grandpa's favorite music, the Jersey Boys, and said, *"I thought we'd go to Dahlonega for ice cream."* One of the things Steve and I enjoyed was taking the one-and-a-half-hour drive there to go to a little ice cream parlor and have ice cream. We always enjoyed the drive, listening to music on the way, and being together. Robby wanted to let me relive that memory, so he had planned this outing. It was such a memorable time for Robby and me; we both reminisced about Grandpa, and there was laughter and tears. He, in his grieving, allowed me to grieve; and we bonded and walked through a portion of our grief together. I will never forget that day.

Celebrating the New

As we discussed in Chapter 1, not all grief stems from the passing of a loved one. We may be grieving because of a divorce, loss of a job, frightening medical diagnosis, or other traumatic loss or experience. The concept of celebrating what is good still stands. It's important to not only mourn the loss of the good things we had but also to look for the good in where we are now.

One example of this is a member of our church who was diagnosed with Parkinson's. He talks about how angry he was when he was first diagnosed—he had recently gotten remarried after several years as a widower and felt as though he was being robbed of the chance to be happy again. As he processed his grief, working with our pastor and a counselor, he realized that he could still be happy if he let go of his own plans about what his life should look like. He began to look for the good in his new scenario. These days, he says he's grateful that, since he can no longer work, he gets to get up and eat an unhurried breakfast with his wife each morning. He comes to the church and volunteers during the week, doing whatever he can to help the Body of Christ. It's not what he imagined his life would be at his age, but it is the life God has given him. He said that learning to be thankful for that and celebrating what he can do rather than pining for the things he can no longer do helps him to have peace and joy, even in his grief.

Preparing to Deal With Loss

> "We're taught how to acquire things, not
> what to do when we lose them."
> –J.W. James & R. Friedman
> *Healthy Grieving*

No one prepares you to deal with loss. There are classes to prepare for most things in life, but no classes to prepare for the emotional upheaval that follows any major loss. Maybe it's because humans don't want to think about the worst until we have to, or maybe it's just because it makes us uncomfortable. Whatever the reason, and in spite of the fact that loss is one of the few universal human experiences, we usually enter grief with few, if any, tools for walking through it healthily.

Not many of us feel qualified to talk about grieving, to try to help someone know how to walk this road, a road we all have to walk in life. I have considered my qualifications to even have an opinion or to write on the topic of grief. I'm not a psychologist or sociologist. I'm not educated by an academic school in the field of grief. I am, however, well acquainted with grieving people and the process of grieving. Whether the grief came from the actions of others, my own choices, or from something that was just a natural part of life, grief and I have been well acquainted.

Throughout my life, I have found that both for myself and those I have spent time with, the only way to get through grief with a peace greater than I or anyone could ever imagine is to walk through it with God.

There are a few telltale signs that you haven't dealt with your grief in a healthy way yet. First, if you don't have anyone you can talk to about the loss or refuse to speak about it with anyone, you may not be handling your grief in a healthy way. Perhaps you are overactive, either at work or in a hobby, so that you can distract yourself from your loss. If you would rather be alone all the time and have begun to isolate yourself from people you care about, this can be a sign that you need to allow God to walk through your grief with you, as can engaging in potentially harmful behavior, such as drinking too much or taking excessive risks. If you are not trying to take care of yourself with your eating and sleeping habits, or you have developed a new tendency to overreact to small events, you may not be handling your grief in a healthy way. Maybe you avoid forming new relationships or getting close to people to minimize your chances of being hurt again.

If you find that you are dealing with several of these behaviors, it might be time for you to talk to a counselor, spiritual leader, or both about your grieving process. Talk, pray, and journal about how you feel. You will never feel a feeling or express your grief in a way that's too difficult for God to handle.

Grief and Recovery

What does it mean to recover from your grief? Often, we want recovery to mean that we don't feel sad anymore. The truth, however, is that after a major loss, you may experience waves of sadness for the rest of your life. This doesn't mean you haven't recovered from your grief. A truth about grief that has been repeated often but was first written by Jamie Anderson in 2014:

Grief, I've learned, is really just love. It's all the love you want to give, but cannot. All that unspent love gathers up in the corners of your eyes, the lump in your throat, and in that hollow part of your chest. Grief is just love with no place to go. (p. 1)

Recovery doesn't mean we stop feeling love for whatever it is that we've lost. Recovering means we learn how to move forward into tomorrow, unfettered by pain from the love we've lost. It means that we can hold onto what has happened to us without it holding us back. It means that fear of being hurt again is no longer keeping others at arm's length. It means you can reflect on fond memories and not be overwhelmed with regret, remorse, or uncontrollable grief.

"How do I know if I've experienced healing?"

The question was asked by a young mother who had just gone through an unexpected divorce after over ten years of marriage. My answer was to begin asking her questions about the divorce, the marriage that had ended, and her current relationships. Healing allows you to talk about the pain you've experienced, the people involved, and the sadness you still face without bitterness. It enables you to move forward in your relationships and love completely, without reservation. It means you can forgive—God, yourself, and others who have hurt you. Recovery doesn't mean that tears never come; it means that you can understand that sometimes tears are a normal part of life. You can give yourself space to be sad, and you have the capacity to be happy.

Healing is a process. Recovery doesn't happen overnight or all at once. But it can happen. The peace and joy that Jesus offered to His disciples in John 14:27 when He said, *"Peace I leave with you; my peace I give you. I do not give to you as the world gives. Do not let your hearts be troubled and do not be afraid"* (NIV) is available to us too.

Staying Open to Grief

One of the ways that we can process grief healthily is to stay open to it. It's so much easier to shut down, to refuse to deal with it. Often, we just want to look away. It's so much easier to face life if we can pretend that the grief isn't there.

Staying open to grief means that we can access the emotions and share them. I had an opportunity to watch our friend Vince doing this one day when Steve and I sat with him and his wife for lunch. As the conversation covered memories of times gone by with laughter and fondness, one of us asked, *"Vince, how is your mom?"* Immediately, his tears came.

We knew that this incredible lady, a centerpiece in so many of the memories we had shared, had Alzheimer's or dementia. Vince's mom was hilarious, loving, and caring. She was the kind of person you fell in love with when you met her, and her relationship with God was remarkable.

That day, however, tears were at the surface as our dear friend spoke about the mom he could still see physically but had lost emotionally to a disease that was gradually destroying the memories she had of years gone past. He was grieving as he and my husband enjoyed sharing stories, but he didn't stop talking about it to look away from the grief. Instead, he stayed open. In doing that, he was able to talk about the way forward—a daughter buying her grandma's house so that the family can continue making memories there, a mother with a deep relationship with God even as her memories are wiped out by her disease.

If he had turned away from his grief and answered with one of the trite phrases we are taught to use: *"It is what it is,"* 'Fine,' *"As good as can be expected,"* and then changed the subject, that part of his heart that processed his grief that day would have remained unhealed. There is no shortcut through our grief, only the plodding steps that take us one step at a time closer to recovering. Openness is one of those steps.

Moving on Without Letting Go

We experience growth as a result of our grief. As we are forced to learn new ways to connect to the world, ways we didn't need before, we have to grow and be open to the new things in our lives. Perhaps it is a stretch for you to relate to the world as a person who has been diagnosed with cancer, or as a widow, or as a divorcée; maybe the unfamiliar thing for you is being retired or fatherless. The list could go on and on because each stretch that we are forced into is a result of whatever our loss has encompassed. However, as we stretch to the new places grief is forcing us into, we are growing emotionally as well. Life keeps changing, and so do we.

Sometimes, as life moves on, we feel as though it's time for us to be 'finished' grieving. That seems to be the way our society works—we are given time to grieve but then expected to get on with life and stop being sad. But in reality, it's important to realize that even as you move forward, it's okay to grieve. You may still experience waves of sadness years after a loss. Overwhelming grief will begin to pass, and you will become accustomed to your loss.

Your life can be good again, even though it won't be the same. You won't be the same, either. Grief will change you. Working through your grief toward healing will enable you to grow—grief will make you stronger, your heart bigger, your compassion powerful, and your spirit indestructible. Refusing to confront your grief will leave you bitter and angry, your heart hardened, and your spirit broken. Sometimes, the next step to healing is to change your perspective.

Reflection

- How has the situation that causes you pain helped you grow?

- What can you celebrate today to help your heart recover from your grief?

5

SHIFTING YOUR PERSPECTIVE

I remember one specific day when the weather reporters were saying it was a stifling day here in Ohio. They were recommending that people stay in the air-conditioning while I was sitting on the porch with the fan on, and it seemed to me that it was lovely and temperate, even mildly cool. There was a light breeze; the birds were chirping and diving for food. Vito, the German Shepherd, was dozing by my side. I looked out from my porch onto a lush, green pasture with horses grazing peacefully. As I chuckled a little at the contrast, it occurred to me that the difference was in my perspective. We were looking at different things, so we had different responses.

Isn't our response to everything in life shaped by the

same thing? We see a glass half full or half empty, the gifts life offers or the burden it brings, inconvenience or opportunity, heartache or celebration.

Earthly or Heavenly Perspective

Romans 8 is a reminder that God's perspective is vastly different than ours. This chapter reminds us continually that our lives need to be centered around the life we have in the spirit rather than the life we have in the body. In this chapter, we find hope, power, and strength.

Courage in the face of suffering isn't the absence of fear but our decision to go forward despite it all, even when we don't want to. The writer of Romans gives us an unapologetic reminder that God is working towards eternity when he says, *"I consider that our present sufferings are not worth comparing with the glory that will be revealed in us"* (v. 18, NIV). When life is hard, when suffering comes, we can rest assured that—in the end, it will all be worth it. More than worth it.

He also tells us that a perspective shift is necessary to live in the peace of God when troubles come:

Those who live according to the flesh have their minds set on what the flesh desires; but those who live in accordance with the Spirit have their minds set on what the Spirit desires. The mind governed by the flesh is death, but the mind governed by the Spirit is life and peace (v. 5–6, NIV).

We have often used this verse to talk about sin. But sometimes your flesh doesn't desire something sinful. Your flesh also desires comfort, ease, and a pain-free life. God knows that ever since the fall of man in Genesis 3, that isn't how life on Earth works. Your flesh will try to convince you that, if God really cared about you and was all-powerful like He says He is, He would provide this trouble-free existence for you. These verses remind us that thinking that way will never lead us to life and peace.

I knew a pastor, Father Chris Coleman, who used to say to his congregations, *"God is good all the time,"* and they would respond with, *"All the time, God is good."* They were working on their perspective. Who do they look to for hope, purpose, strength, and love? They were reminding themselves to look at You. We are more than conquerors in You. Regardless of our circumstances, this body, this world, and these circumstances are temporary.

You say that if You, God, are for us, who can be against us? You give us an understanding of Your incredible love and protection for our hearts, minds, and souls throughout every verse in this Romans chapter. You are telling us that just as Father Chris Coleman was empowered, His message to all who met Him was that they were empowered too.

Our permanent home is heaven, not Earth. There is nothing in this world that can change that fact. Jesus put it plainly in John 14:

I Am the Way, and the Truth, and the Life: Let not your hearts be troubled. Believe in God; believe also in me. In my Father's house are many rooms. If it were not so, would I have told you that I go to prepare a place for you? And if I go and prepare a place for you, I will come again and will take you to myself, that where I am you may be also (v. 1–3, ESV).

There are times when it looks foolish to say that God is good all the time. There are moments of loss when everything inside of us screams that a good, loving God would not have allowed this much pain to happen. In those moments, we need the courage to immerse ourselves in the Word of God, where we can find reassurance and peace.

If we go back to Romans 8, we can see that the whole chapter, all the reassurances of God's love for us, His reminder that we are more than conquerors through Him, all of these are set before us as truth based on the first few verses. These verses remind us that the reason all of that is true is that Jesus, with His eyes on eternity, suffered on the cross to allow us to inherit all of these promises. His suffering changed everything for us when we look at it through the lens of eternity.

Nancy Guthrie puts it this way in her book *Hearing Jesus Speak Into Your Sorrow* (2009):

While he cares deeply about us and the physical pain we experience, he cares far more about our spiritual conditions. He knows that these bodies of ours are wearing out and will die before the day comes when he raises them up and renews them. It's our souls that he is most concerned about. There is something more important to Jesus than our bodily comfort and safety (p. 60).

God Is Sovereign

These ideas were put to the test by Father Chris's three congregations when, after a game of golf, a car accident claimed his life at the age of fifty. So many people were hurting and saddened by the loss of a beloved shepherd in their church. For many, they had lost a treasured friend; others felt the loss of a man who had been a source of strength and grace. His words, *"God is good all the time,"* would need to include even the days, weeks, and years after his death.

At times like these, it can be difficult to balance grief and celebration of the goodness of God. The quest for the wisdom to correctly shift our perspective was necessary in the face of this tragic death, but it is also paramount in so many other undeniable heartaches and devastating life or health challenges. Only God has the answers when we are suffering.

When tragedy strikes, we can remember that, although we need to grieve, we can mourn with the hope and understanding that the Lord holds our hearts in His hands. Jesus has come to bring hope, even in grief. In Luke 4, Jesus was invited to read a portion of Scripture in the synagogue. He opened the scroll of Isaiah, and found this passage:

The Spirit of the Sovereign Lord is on me,
because the Lord has anointed me
to proclaim good news to the poor.
He has sent me to bind up the brokenhearted,
to proclaim freedom for the captives
and release from darkness for the prisoners,
to proclaim the year of the Lord's favor
and the day of vengeance of our God,
to comfort all who mourn... (61:1–2, NIV)

Then He said to them, "Today this Scripture has been fulfilled in your hearing" (Luke 4:22, NIV). Comfort... Jesus offers comfort when we mourn.

God has a plan and purpose for each of our lives. Even when, from an earthly perspective, a life ends too soon, as Father Chris's life did, God is working. Father Chris had the opportunity to bring God's love, grace, mercy, and joy to many people. He helped to give everyone he met and interacted with a new perspective.

He gave hope to those who struggled and who mourned. He brought joy and laughter to all he met. Then, his race was done. It was time for him to pass the baton.

In His sovereignty, God designs a life with a beginning and an endpoint. At that endpoint, there is someone waiting to take the baton and run with it. Remember that His perspective is eternal—He is most concerned with our souls. Out of the ashes of our sorrow can come beauty. That's what the very next verse in this passage of Isaiah says:

... and provide for those who grieve in Zion—
to bestow on them a crown of beauty
instead of ashes,
the oil of joy
instead of mourning,
and a garment of praise
instead of a spirit of despair.
They will be called oaks of righteousness,
a planting of the Lord
for the display of his splendor (61: 3, NIV).

Wow, God doesn't promise small, does He? His promise isn't *"I'll make you okay again; you'll still be broken but not too badly."* It's beauty for ashes, joy for mourning, praise for despair. And at the end of it, he tells us that we will display His splendor in this way. The glory of God shines through the young widow who finds joy again, the terminal patient with peace, or the bereaved parent who can praise through their tears.

In every situation, God is sovereign. His Word promises us that if we hold onto Him, we will overcome everything that life can throw at us. Looking again at Romans 8, we can see this promise, *"No, in all these things we are more than conquerors through him who loved us"* (v. 37). More than conquerors? Even the promise lets us know that there will be a battle. The battle that is waged on our hearts has eternal consequences, and God wants to make sure we know that with Him, we can win.

Feelings Can't Be Supreme

Our circumstances or emotions, although they are valid, cannot be the place where our hearts find rest. Our rest is in our relationship with God. We can look past those things that often entangle us to what He would have us do despite how we feel about it. Recognizing the sovereignty of God helps us to see how we can be a light in the darkness and bring hope to others despite the pain we face. When we don't let our feelings rule us, we can be the instruments of love and peace, even in our suffering.

That doesn't mean we need to invalidate or ignore our feelings. It just means we need to put them in their rightful place—submitted to the sovereignty of God.

This sounds difficult, and it is. It sounds unkind, like God is uncaring of how we feel. But this is not the truth —actually, the opposite is true. Jesus assures us in John 16 that trusting Him will produce peace:

I have told you these things, so that in Me you may have [perfect] peace and confidence. In the world, you have tribulation and trials and distress and frustration;

but be of good cheer [take courage; be confident, certain, undaunted]! For I have overcome the world. [I have deprived it of power to harm you and have conquered it for you] (v. 33).

Do you see it? Far from not caring about our feelings, Jesus is lighting the path for us to feel peace. He reminds us that we will have troubles, but assures us that He has already overcome the world so that we can live at peace even in the middle of those troubles.

There are times when we don't want to follow the path God sets out in His Word—the path of trusting His sovereignty rather than giving our emotions the reins. It can seem unfair. It's important to remember, however, that the instructions of God always lead us to the best possible path for us. He won't lead us down a road where we will be miserable. God leads us to deal with our emotions, believe His Word, and trust Him because He knows that is the path to peace and healing. He knows that when we trust Him with even our deepest sorrows and most difficult experiences, we will enjoy the peace He spoke about in John 16.

So often, we get mired in the emotions and trials of today and forget that God is there in the midst of it all. Listen to His still, small voice saying, *"You can do it; you are empowered to overcome the emotions. You have the power to climb to the summit. You just must believe that with Me, partnered arm in arm, you can do all things—big or small—with love, mercy, grace, kindness, strength, and power."*

Giving From a Grateful Heart

Gratitude is something that has helped me immeasurably in bringing my feelings in line with God's Word. There are times that your heart will tell you that you can't be grateful in this circumstance or while carrying this pain. But even though we can't be thankful for every circumstance that comes our way, we can be thankful in them. This is what Paul wrote in 1 Thessalonians, when he said, *"Rejoice always, pray continually, give thanks in all circumstances; for this is God's will for you in Christ Jesus"* (5:16–18, NIV).

When we are able to give thanks to God for His blessings, even in the midst of turmoil and pain, God can use us to bless others, which blesses us in turn. An example of this is Steve's friend, John.

John lived in Cincinnati, and we lived in Atlanta. He called Steve one day and said he needed to see Steve. We knew we would be heading to Cincinnati to see Steve's mom soon, and Steve told John that he would let him know when we were heading there. A few days before our arrival, John's father passed away. The funeral was the morning that he and Steve planned to meet. Of course, Steve told him we'd be back another time and offered to postpone their meeting. John declined, saying that God had put it on his heart to give Steve something. Even in the midst of his own grief, John came to meet with Steve.

John had been blessed by a book called *Waking The Dead* by John Eldredge. He was grateful that this book had been such a blessing to him, and he knew God wanted him to pass it on to Steve. Steve had read it before, but he knew there must be a reason for this book to be important in his heart at that specific time. So Steve read that book cover to cover, chapter by chapter, paragraph by paragraph, line by line. It transformed his life.

Because he was in the right place to receive what the book had to offer, he understood all of the pain in his heart and brokenness from years of family challenges, divorce, and business defeats. He realized he had been waiting to recover and become whole-hearted again. He went to a boot camp that John Eldredge led. Wild at Heart Ministries, as it is now called, changed his life.

After this experience, Steve was passionate about men with broken hearts, because he knew their pain. He gave away over a thousand *Waking the Dead* books and workbooks over the next four years. He took many hundreds of men through that book, reading aloud with them individually or in a group, working with them to experience healing. John's gift of reaching out in the midst of his own grief set Steve's heart free to choose recovery, and then Steve also chose to give, even in the midst of his own pain.

Even while undergoing chemotherapy treatment, Steve still met with the men and worked through this book with them. One gentleman he went through the book with during the last few months of his life was so impacted by it and by their time of dealing with pain and grief that he was able to realize he had fallen into addiction. He started AA and recovery because of it.

It is truly in giving, especially in the middle of our grief, that we receive. We receive peace, hope, love, and joy in our giving. Without gratitude, grief can make us feel as though someone else owes us something. Gratitude reminds us that we are already blessed, no matter what our situation currently is.

Forgiveness Allows Healing

"Forgiveness is the key that unlocks the door of resentment and the handcuffs of hatred. It is a power that breaks the chains of bitterness and the shackles of selfishness." –Corrie Ten Boom

Few people have recorded their journey to forgiveness as well as Corrie Ten Boom. She and her family were prisoners in the Nazi prison camps. She lost several family members during this time, and she herself was the target of unspeakable cruelty. After the war, she returned to the Netherlands and started a Christian camp on the site of a former concentration camp to help refugees and former prisoners experience healing. She spoke throughout her life about the power of God to enable His people to forgive, reminding her listeners that God doesn't just instruct us to forgive, He also enables us to do it.

_____

Forgive Others

_____

"I will never forgive him."

How often do we hear this in the context of an awful offense? When our suffering is the direct result of the actions of others, forgiveness becomes a hurdle that our society says we don't need to jump across. But God's way is different.

We are commanded to forgive; in fact, Matthew 6:15 states that we cannot be forgiven if we refuse to forgive. That can feel like a hard pill to swallow when someone has caused you intense pain. Again, we have to believe that God is telling us to do something because He knows it will be better for us. There is a saying that refusing to forgive is like *"swallowing poison and expecting the other person to die"* (Evans & Sullivan, 1995). God knows this. Holding onto our anger and resentment will kill us, not them.

Forgiveness doesn't mean the other person hasn't wronged you. In fact, you can't forgive without naming the offense. Forgiveness admits that there was a wrong done and that the fallout from it has been hurtful, even catastrophic. Forgiveness then proceeds to release the desire for vengeance. When we have forgiven someone, we no longer wish for them to suffer as we have suffered. We wish healing for them as well as for ourselves.

Forgive Ourselves

One of our church friends' daughters, Tara, was a bright, cheerful college student. She was kind and generous and often went out of her way to do things for others. At the ministry she was part of, she broke down to the college pastor one day. It had been two years since the death of her aunt. This aunt had led her to Christ; she had been the only Christian in their family until Tara got saved.

"I just can't forgive myself. It's my fault she died," Tara sobbed.

As the minister asked questions to find out why she felt responsible, Tara told the story. One day while Tara was still in high school, she wasted time with her friends after school, playing around instead of going straight to the area where she was supposed to get on the school bus. Not surprisingly, she missed her bus home. Tara's mom was an emotionally abusive, angry woman, and Tara was hesitant to call her to pick her up and risk getting yelled at. So she called her aunt instead. The aunt had quickly agreed to come and get her, but she hadn't ever shown up; on the way to the school, she was in a fatal accident.

Tara had been unable to rid herself of the persistent belief that her aunt's death was her fault. No one else understood; no one knew her aunt had been on the way to pick her up. Beneath her happy exterior, Tara was suffering well beyond what anyone realized. She had begun harming herself purposefully, getting drunk alone in her dorm room, and going days without food sometimes to punish herself. Although she hadn't done anything wrong, her choices had led to the death of one of the people she held most dear. Tara needed to forgive herself for the choices she had made, or she was going to wreck her life.

Whether our grief is the result of innocent choices—like Tara's was—or sinful choices, we often struggle to forgive ourselves when our suffering or the suffering of others can be laid at our door. The Bible tells us that God has removed our sins from us *"as far as the east is from the west"* (Psalm 103:12), but even so, it can be difficult for us to stop holding onto them.

Tara's minister led her through five steps to forgive herself. If you are struggling to forgive yourself because you feel that your mistakes have led to your suffering or the suffering of others, these steps may be helpful to you, too.

First, write down the story of what happened the way it actually happened, not the way that the guilt wants you to remember it. Next, divide your actions into three categories—unethical, unwise, and unknowing. Unethical actions are wrong. Unwise actions are things that were not thought out well ahead of time. Unknowing actions are neutral actions that you had no idea could lead to a bad outcome. Then, take responsibility, repent, and make amends if possible for your unethical actions; learn from your unwise actions; and let go of the guilt from your unknowing actions.

Forgiving yourself isn't pretending like you didn't do anything wrong. It's acknowledging the wrong and choosing not to let guilt or shame from your past actions dictate your future.

Shifting your perspective to focus on the eternal, remembering the sovereignty of God even in the bad, redirecting your emotions with gratitude, and practicing forgiveness can help you navigate through your grief and grow through your trials.

Reflection

- How can you practice gratitude for the gifts God has given you, even while acknowledging your loss?

- What steps of forgiveness do you need to take today to forgive yourself or others for causing pain?

6

BITTER OR BETTER

There are times when life is not only challenging but also downright unfair. Suffering is painful, cruel, and even devastating. There are no exceptions to this. That acquaintance who appears to have a life free of trouble is not exempt. Someone else's life may seem easy to you, but they have had, are having, or will have tragedies and pain that affect them.

I knew a woman named Kim who seemed to have a charmed life. Her husband was kind and attentive, her children were healthy and had grown into strong Christians with healthy families of their own, and her financial situation was solid. Acquaintances envied the ease with which she seemed to skate through life without sorrow. None of them knew that, as a child, she was cruelly abused, then entered foster care and went through multiple foster homes without being adopted. She aged out of foster care and was diagnosed with a health condition that stemmed from those early years of abuse and neglect. She had been married before to an abusive man who left her for another woman.

To know Kim was to love her; she was a beautiful soul. She was patient, kind, and loving. She brought joy to everyone around her. No one would ever have guessed that she had suffered so much. She had not allowed her tragedies to make her bitter. She had not stayed broken. She chose to allow the Holy Spirit to do His work in her, using the sorrow in her life to mold her into the person God made her to be.

We each have a choice—allow God to use our circumstance or situation to make us stronger and better, or allow our pain to make us bitter and broken. No one but us can choose our response to our circumstances. It is our choice alone.

A World at War

It's important to remember that there is a war going on. It has gone on since before the foundation of the world. Satan set himself up against God long ago, and every trial we encounter, every sorrow that burdens us is an outflow of that war. Let's go back to Genesis 3, to the beginning of the war on humanity…

Now the serpent was more crafty than any other beast of the field that the Lord God had made.

He said to the woman, "Did God actually say, You shall not eat of any tree in the garden?" And the woman said to the serpent, "We may eat of the fruit of the trees in the garden, but God said, 'You shall not eat of the fruit of the tree that is in the midst of the garden, neither shall you touch it, lest you die." But the serpent said to the woman, "You will not surely die. For God knows that when you eat of it your eyes will be opened, and you will be like God, knowing good and evil" (v. 1–5, ESV).

Adam and Eve didn't come up with the plan to eat from the one forbidden tree on their own. They had an adversary; Satan hated God, so of course, he hated humans made in the image of God. So he cast doubt on God's character—not His love, but His character. Satan was casting doubt on whether they could trust that God had their best interests at heart. How often does he do the same with us?

Satan sowed doubt using questions about whether God was denying them something pleasant, or withholding knowledge from them. He told them that the thing God wasn't allowing them to have was actually the thing they needed. His goal was to convince them that God was being selfish—and the next verse tells us that it worked! Eve was easily convinced that God was holding out on her, and she convinced Adam. They trusted Satan instead of God.

Satan's pride had caused him to set himself up against God. Ezekiel 28 records how Satan became proud, how he desired the glory and praise that was due to God, and how he was cast out of heaven to Earth. In Eden, Satan inspired that same pride in Eve. She could be like God, he said, simply by doing what she wanted to do instead of what God told her to do. Pride is the mother of all sin and conflict.

They could have chosen differently, but they became unwitting pawns in Satan's war on God by believing the lies the enemy told them instead of the truth of God. Adam and Eve gave Satan power over their lives by succumbing to the temptation to be like God. They gave him control over their lives, the Earth, and everyone who would ever walk on it. They opened the door to pain, suffering, illness, disease, poverty, hunger, greed, and violence. These came with Adam and Eve's choice to believe Satan instead of God.

Because of this, we are all born into the war between God and Satan. The thoroughness with which the effects of this war would permeate our lives is anticipated in the judgment that God pronounces on each of the partici- pants in the scene in Genesis 3:1–5. No area of human life will be untouched. The effects of sin will touch their bodies through pain and death, their relationships, and their work.

God didn't leave them without hope. Even in the judgment, He pronounces over them at the end of Genesis 3. He tells them that through humanity will come the weapon that will finish Satan. In a divine plot twist, the death blow to the enemy will come from the woman Satan targeted with his lies. Throughout the Old and New Testaments, from Genesis to Revelation, the war is described, and so is the victory.

Before Jesus came, mankind was still in captivity, but Jesus rising from the dead destroyed the power of Satan over all of humanity, bringing us back to free will. This is why Jesus began His public ministry with the reading from Isaiah 61. He had come to set us free, to set in motion the events that will end the war and destroy the enemy once and for all.

The key is to see our pain from the perspective of a vast cosmic war that all of humanity was brought into by Adam and Eve. Satan revels in our pain and would love to keep us mired in it for the rest of our lives—and eternity, if possible. God suffers with us, and He offers us relief from our suffering if we will trust Him. Who will we trust? Will we believe the lies as Eve did? Or will we believe that God has our best interests at heart and that we can trust that He is working out His perfect plan even in the middle of the brokenness that is an inherent part of living in a war zone?

Ways to Win

Paul reminds us in Ephesians 6 that we are in a war. He also reminds us who we are fighting:

Finally, be strong in the Lord and in the strength of his might. Put on the whole armor of God, so that you may be able to stand against the schemes of the devil. For we do not wrestle against flesh and blood, but against the rulers, against the authorities, against the cosmic powers over this present darkness, against the spiritual forces of evil in the heavenly places. Therefore take up the whole armor of God, that you may be able to withstand in the evil day, and having done all, to stand firm. Stand therefore, having fastened on the belt of truth, and having put on the breastplate of righteousness, and, as shoes for your feet, having put on the readiness given by the gospel of peace. In all circumstances take up the shield of faith, with which you can extinguish all the flaming darts of the evil one; and take the helmet of salvation, and the sword of the Spirit, which is the word of God, praying at all times in the Spirit, with all prayer and supplication (v. 10–18).

Our battle is not with our neighbor, spouse, or children; the battle is between Satan and God in heavenly places. We need to remember who we are fighting against. Satan uses us when we let him; he uses our emotions and circumstances to steal, kill, and destroy. Even when we are grieving, our words and actions matter. God sent the Holy Spirit to be with us, strengthen us, empower us, and give us wisdom. When we put on God's spiritual armor, we are ready to battle against our enemy.

Spiritual Weapons

God gives us step-by-step instructions for winning the war in the Spirit. If we're ever unsure of what we should do in a situation or if we forget any of His instructions, we are to remember the two greatest commands: *"Love the Lord your God with all your heart and with all your mind and with all your soul and with all your strength"* and *"You shall love your neighbor as yourself"* (Mark 12:30–31, ESV). We are to love God and be a reflection of His love for our neighbor.

Wait, you might be thinking. I thought we were talking about the war between God and Satan. We are! Love is the battle plan that Jesus laid out for us.

Loving people, even when they hurt us, is not the

most likely battle plan to come to our natural mind. But here is where we come back to remembering who our enemy is. The war is to be waged against the enemy of our souls, not the people around us. The battle plan can't include seeing our fellow humans as the enemy. We should see the broken people around us, those whose failures bring us pain, as hostages in the war that encompasses the whole Earth. And if they are hostages, they are not the ones we are fighting against. So we love them, hoping and praying that God's love will break through the chains that bind them.

I want to add a side note here. Love is an all-inclusive command, but allowing others to mistreat you isn't. If you are in a relationship with an abusive or toxic person, look for an opportunity to leave. God's requirement of love does not require you to stay in a relationship like that. You will need to forgive them. Admit the abuse and the damage it caused and release the desire for vengeance. It's not easy, but God will empower you to do it.

We didn't pay the price to win the war; God did. He is the one who understands the cost of winning. Jesus, more than any of us, understands the cost of love, our most valuable weapon against the enemy. When Satan steals our health, we continue loving God and others. When he tries to kill us, we continue loving God and others. When he comes to destroy us, we continue loving God and others.

We are told to love God with all our heart, mind, soul, and strength and to love our neighbors. This applies to the friendly neighbors and the not-so-nice ones, the easy-to-love and our enemies, the young and the old, the homeless and the well-to-do. These are the ones we are meant to love. When we don't know how to love, we have the Holy Spirit that will step in for us. He will love through us, especially when we believe we have nothing left to give. We must simply ask Him. This love compels us to let go of our hurt, pain, and pride. This love allows us to be the opposite of Eve in the garden. We can surrender and, like Christ in Gethsemane, whisper, *"Not my will but Yours."* In learning to love, we become stronger and better instead of broken and bitter.

Love expresses and releases God's power in an amazing way. When we love, we are free, truly free of all the ugly and painful results of being bitter and broken. God can heal, strengthen and make our broken places whole again, making us stronger and better. In this way, we do not have to be prisoners of the bitterness that, if left unchecked, will overshadow everything we do. We can be free to be all God has created us to be.

Freedom to Choose

No one would be foolish enough to say life is easy, because sometimes it is not. But we are not alone. We have the Holy Spirit to guide, encourage, strengthen, and empower us. He gives us grace that is beyond our human understanding. I know because I've been there. And when I was there, at the hardest points of my life, so was the Holy Spirit.

This world is far from perfect. Some people are unabashedly self-serving; some are angry and cruel. Bad things can and do happen to good people. God has given everyone the freedom to choose their thoughts, words, and actions. God, in His love, risked rejection and pain to give each of us the freedom to choose Him wholeheartedly. God cannot take away the freedom to choose from those who would use it wrongly. True love doesn't work that way, and it can't. True love does not force love in return.

God created mankind with the freedom to choose. We can't force people to love, be kind, or do the right thing. It's not possible. Fortunately, this also means that we have the freedom to choose to allow God to heal our hearts from the pain and tragedy we have faced in life.

But not everyone will choose this. Some people will

use their freedom to hurt others. We need to see the bigger picture, focusing on God and His Word. In this way, we will find peace in the midst of turmoil.

Heavenly Home

This world is not our permanent home. We are sojourners—which is to say, we are temporary residents here on this Earth. We are traveling through this world, heading for our true home in heaven.

Jesus reassured us of this when He said, *"There are many rooms in my Father's house. I wouldn't tell you this unless it was true. I am going there to prepare a place for each of you"* (John 14:2 CEV).

Our time on Earth is short compared to eternity. Our goal can't be to get comfortable here in this world. Perhaps this is part of the reason God allows trials to come our way, to remind us not to get too comfortable here. This is why a perspective shift that focuses our eyes on the eternal is so helpful.

Our purpose on Earth is to reflect our Heavenly Father's love on the world around us. He uses all our personalities, weaknesses, and strengths to be God's hands, feet, and hearts here on Earth.

Reflection

- Today are you willing to trust and follow the One who loved you?

- How can you express love to the people around you?

7
_____

THE JOURNEY

The book of Exodus records the escape of God's people out of slavery in Egypt. God used Moses to lead His people to the land He had promised them. They had been enslaved for four hundred years in spite of the fact that God had promised their ancestors that He would give them their own land. Even though God led them, they had to make the journey through the wilderness to the land God promised. Their disobedience caused that journey to take much longer than God originally intended it to take.

Isn't that the way it sometimes is with us? God is leading us on a journey toward His promises of peace, joy, love, and healing. When we hold onto our anger and bitterness, or when we don't allow God into our grief, the journey toward healing begins to feel long and hard.

It is taking the time to grieve that can bring healing from the inside out. There are times we can do it alone; in fact, sometimes we need to be alone with our Heavenly Father in our sadness and grief. Then there are other times when we need someone else to help clear the riverbed of our hearts, helping us move the boulders and tree trunks that have cluttered the free flow of God's restoring and healing Spirit. However we need to grieve, we must let God into the places that only He can heal.

Sometimes, grief comes at the end of a long, hard battle. Maybe we fought against the circumstance that brings grief, and when the battle is done we're finally in a position to allow ourselves to grieve the thing that wasn't able to come to pass. When we are forced to stop fighting, and the battle is finished, there is sadness for the lost dreams, both our dreams and the dreams of the people we love.

We are then confronted with the fallout from the battle, the debris left on the landscape of our lives and the lives of those we love. When the battle is done, we are in a position to realize that while some people stood and fought with us, others abandoned us out on the battlefield. When the fighting is over, we can see the wounds from those we trusted that betrayed us. The battle is a great revealer of who walks with us—we will look back over it and see hidden treasures that we once overlooked. We will also see the ravaged, hollow carcasses of once-treasured relationships.

There is only one place that I know that is safe enough to go with grief: God.

A Journey of Healing

For me, it was going to a retreat in Colorado that unearthed my deep need to grieve. God didn't reveal my need to me in the people or even the messages. It was during my time in the prayer room that God met me face-to-face.

Suddenly, I saw that I needed to forgive God for allowing some of the things that had happened over the last several years. I would never have had the audacity to think I should even consider needing to forgive God. But He knew. It was the beginning of the healing in my heart.

God, in His gracious love, continued what He started in Colorado. He knew that I needed to stop compartmentalizing my heart. I had been using this tactic to survive, but God didn't want me to just survive; He wanted me to thrive, and to do that He knew I needed to be healed. I wasn't ready to look this reality in the face, so I withdrew.

I believed I needed better tools for dealing with my grief. God said, *"No, you need healing for your grief, the grief you don't even realize is still there."* He knew that this pain, if left unchecked and unchallenged in my heart, would eventually take me out. The wounds in my heart were deep, and I had covered over them. It was as though I had been shot, and the wound had closed with the bullet still in it. It was only a matter of time until that festering wound caused me serious problems.

He needed to do surgery on those wounds. They were deep, mortal wounds that only He could heal. The picture that He showed me in my heart was that of a surgeon cutting out the infected area, and God pouring gold into the clean open wound to sear it and keep it clean and pure. The gold was visible, showing that there was an injury, but it was a weakness that would now become a strength. It would be stronger than anything I could have accomplished. My healing would become a glaring shield; it would always remind me—and my enemy— who I was and whose I was. It was painful but complete.

We must walk back through the battlefield to find the treasures and bury the carcasses so that we can fully heal, be stronger than before, and be able to embark on the next leg of our journey. Psalm 23 expresses this truth beautifully:

He makes me lie down in green pastures.
He leads me beside still waters.
He restores my soul.

He leads me in paths of righteousness
for his name's sake.

Even though I walk through the valley of the shadow
of death,
I will fear no evil,
for you are with me;
your rod and your staff,
they comfort me (v.2–4, ESV).

God is the true safe place. He will never leave you or forsake you. He will always be your Healer, Master, Good Shepherd, and Loving Father.

Many years ago, I came upon a prayer from Christian Recovery. It simply says, *"God grant me the courage to not turn away from You until I have faced You squarely, without excuse or explanation, but naked with all my weaknesses and strengths."* I have regularly prayed this ever since. It is in identifying my weaknesses and strengths with God that I am helped. That's when He makes me stronger and heals my heart. Allowing God into those places, remembering that He is a safe place even in my grief, is the journey of healing that we each must take.

Journeying Through Truth

Truth is the key to recovery. When we are grieving the loss of someone, it's easy to sweep aside parts of the truth about them. In doing that, we will have a skewed viewpoint. We will either remember them as better than they were or worse.

A friend of mine lost a child at the age of nine in a horrific car accident. Several years later, she had another baby. She went to counseling after saying to her five-year-old one day, *"Your sister never would have done something like that!"* After she calmed down, she realized that the sister had, in fact, done the exact same thing when she was in kindergarten. My friend realized that she had idealized her child who had passed away, and that it was damaging her relationship with her living daughter.

The other side of the coin is the loss of someone with whom you have a bad relationship. You may find it easier to forget the good times and focus solely on the bad things that you remember about them. Unfortunately, this can cause you to be unable to process your natural grief over the loss.

It is important in the grieving process to acknowledge the truth about the person or relationship you have lost and to look for ways to complete that relationship. Look for the places where the relationship feels unfinished. Did you have things you wanted to say? Maybe you wish you had expressed your love, or perhaps the final conversation you had with your lost loved one was hurtful on one or both sides. Completing this relationship might include things like writing the person who passed away a letter or going to their gravesite and saying your unsaid things aloud. This concept is covered in depth in *The Grief Recovery Handbook* by Russell Friedman and John James, and I encourage you to go through that book if you feel that it would be helpful to you.

The Path

As we walk the path of dealing with our grief, it's important to remember to keep learning along the way. Every circumstance and person that comes our way is a potential teacher. We will learn many things, but the most important thing we will learn is how God will always be right there.

A friend told me the story about her sister Angie. Angie had suffered three miscarriages. After the third one, she just never got pregnant again. Her grief hardened within her like a knot in the pit of her stomach, always present. She was angry—angry at herself for not being able to carry a child to term, angry at anyone who was pregnant, and most of all, angry at God for not answering her prayers for a child. Sitting at a church function that was geared towards high school students one day, she listened as the speaker began to talk about how she had been unable to have children, and how she had come close to losing her faith in God. The speaker teared up as she said, *"I don't even know why I'm telling this story. It's not in my notes. It doesn't fit with what I planned to say. But for some reason God wanted me to share it. He wanted someone here to know He is here. He listens. He cares. And you are not alone."* Tears coursed down Angie's face as she heard these words. The reminder that God was with her, even when she was angry with Him, brought a balm of peace to her heart.

If we refuse to hear the lessons that our grief has for us, we won't be able to grow. There is a short poem by Robert Browning Hamilton that expresses what I mean perfectly:

I walked a mile with Pleasure;
She chatted all the way;
But left me none the wiser
For all she had to say.
I walked a mile with Sorrow;
And ne'er a word said she;
But, oh! The things I learned from her,
When Sorrow walked with me (Miller, 2019).

Along the path of grief, we will also need to adapt. As the storms of circumstance come, the way gets darker. We need to adjust our eyes to our new conditions. Beauty is still there. It's just harder to see.

There is a story about a woman named Sedona Schnebly, the wife of one of the founders of the town of Sedona in Arizona in the late 1800s. The Schnebly family was known for their hospitality, offering to lodge newcomers and often hosting community get-togethers at their homestead. Sedona was chosen as the town's namesake because the founders agreed that she would be a fitting symbol of the community. Then in 1905, Sedona's daughter Pearl was killed tragically in an accident while riding a pony shortly before her sixth birthday. Sedona was present but unable to save her. After Pearl's death, Sedona would spend hours standing at the kitchen window, looking out at the grave of her daughter, haunted by feelings of guilt and helplessness.

After months of this, her husband took his family and left the area in an attempt to save his wife from her depression. Sedona returned to the town that bore her name many years later in 1931. There she taught Sunday school and raised funds for the Wayside Chapel, which was finished and dedicated in her honor in 1950 just months before she passed away. Her body was laid next to her daughter's, and their graves can still be seen years later (Collins, 2021).

Sedona had to physically leave the place where she had sustained such a tragic loss to find a way to see the beauty in life again. Her eyes were darkened by her grief until it became all she could see. However, in her later years, she was remembered as a kindhearted and spirited woman and a dedicated Christian. What a beautiful picture of the restoration that God offers us when we turn to Him in our grief, as Sedona did.

It takes courage to work through our grief. There will be days when our hearts just want to forget what has happened and pretend to be fine. Only when we are willing to look our loss in the face can we continue walking the path God had for us whole and healed.

How Compassion and Love Help Us Heal

Grief that is hidden, that doesn't get to be expressed, can turn to anger or bitterness in our hearts. The difficult part about this is that we are culturally wired to *"get over it"* quickly so that we don't make other people uncomfortable by sharing our grief.

When we sweep our grief under the rug, whether it's for our own comfort or the comfort of others, we undermine the process that God has for us to go through with Him. His process will refine us and bring out love and compassion far beyond what we would be able to have without Him. It will enable us to give and receive compassion. God is working in us to make us more like Himself.

Our grief and suffering allow us to connect with others who are experiencing the same things as we have experienced. This compassionate love for others only happens inside of us when we have felt our own grief, not pushed it away, but experienced it and allowed God to heal our hearts from it.

One of the hallmarks of Jesus' ministry on Earth was compassion. Nowhere is this shown more clearly than in Matthew 14. Jesus' cousin, John the Baptist, was in Herod's prison. At the beginning of the chapter, we learn that Herod executed John by beheading him. Remember, this is a family member of Jesus, and a friend and fellow worker in the Kingdom of God. Surely Jesus felt grief over John's death. Here is His response:

As soon as Jesus heard the news, he left in a boat to a remote area to be alone. But the crowds heard where he was headed and followed on foot from many towns. Jesus saw the huge crowd as he stepped from the boat, and he had compassion on them and healed their sick (v. 13–14, NIV).

Jesus felt the need to be alone. He wanted to sit with His grief over the death of John. But then, when the boat got to their destination, hundreds of people had come to meet Him. And out of His grief, He ministered to them. Notice the Bible doesn't say He was irritated that they had followed Him. It doesn't record that He wished they weren't there. It says He felt compassion for them. The word compassion comes from the Latin words pati, meaning *"to suffer"* and com, meaning *"with"* (Lilius, J. et al, 2011). Jesus felt their suffering with them, even in His own suffering. Compassion allows us, His people, to be like Him in this way.

As we see in Matthew, Jesus' compassion led to action on His part. He didn't just feel badly for them. His feeling of suffering with them allowed Him to enter into their suffering and help them. Compassion has the same effect on us. True compassion will help if it can.

Compassion happens inside of us when we stay open to our grief instead of looking for quick fixes to shut it down. We can't rush this process. We can't try to *"fix"* our grief with compassionate action. True compassion is only expressed after suffering is endured.

The Lord Is My Shepherd

We must stop running from our emotions and spend time with God. Quieting ourselves before the Lord needs to be a daily occurrence for us. King David understood this well from the time he was young.

The Message version of Psalm 23 captures the peace of a heart that trusts in God so powerfully:
God, my shepherd!
I don't need a thing.

You have bedded me down in lush meadows,

you find me quiet pools to drink from.

True to your word,

you let me catch my breath

and send me in the right direction (v. 1–3).

David, a shepherd in his youth, understood the role of a shepherd. As a good shepherd, he knew everything there was to know about each individual sheep in his flock. He knew where the best fields to graze and rest his sheep were. The shepherd knew where the still, safe waters were. He knew how to lead his flock and keep them healthy and safe. The shepherd was the owner of the sheep. Unlike a servant, the shepherd would give his life for even one of his sheep. A shepherd's entire life was bound up in the lives of his flock. They were his sheep, and he would die if necessary to protect them.

This is how David viewed God, his shepherd. David knew that he could trust God as much as the sheep trusted him. He knew that God had always provided wisdom, strength, and courage when he wasn't sure what to do. David knew that he could trust God to help him when he prayed. He could put himself into God's hands and not be afraid. Because David knew God's character, love, and commitment to him; he trusted God unconditionally.

In John 10, Jesus refers to Himself as the Good Shepherd. Paul refers to Jesus as *"The God of peace... our*

Lord, Jesus That Great Shepherd" in Hebrews 13:20. Peter states that when *"The Chief Shepherd appears, you will receive a crown of glory that will never fade away"* in 1 Peter 5:4.

Jesus paid the price for us so we would no longer be slaves owned by our circumstances and our grief. We now have the freedom to choose to walk away from them and follow Jesus instead of staying stuck. We now have the freedom to choose to believe God instead of our enemy. He purchased that freedom for us when He died on the cross.

Psalm 23 goes on to say:

Even when the way goes through

Death Valley,

I'm not afraid

when you walk at my side.

Your trusty shepherd's crook

makes me feel secure (v. 4).

When we follow the shepherd, we find peace, even in the middle of difficulty, because we know and are confident in God's character. We know He will walk through the most difficult situations with us. He guides us through perilous times with His wisdom, strength, and courage. When our eyes are fixed on Him and we choose to have Him close to our side, we are led through whatever comes our way safely and in peace and grace. There is security and a sense of comfort in knowing God is always there.

Sometimes we get caught up in the daily grind and forget to stay connected to God. Maybe we start slipping a little too far from the Shepherd's voice, or we just start wandering and daydreaming. We look at the glittery things of this world, and they draw us subtly away from our Good Shepherd. Jesus is there, with His shepherd's rod, the Holy Spirit, to give us a nudge. With that still, small voice, He reminds us where we are and where we need to be. We need to not only hear that voice but also choose to follow it.

The last part of Psalm 23 goes on to say:

You serve me a six-course dinner
right in front of my enemies.
You revive my drooping head;
my cup brims with blessing.
Your beauty and love chase after me
every day of my life.
I'm back home in the house of God
for the rest of my life. (v. 5–6)

There is no greater revenge on the enemy of our souls than to live at peace. There is enormous satisfaction in knowing that no one has the power to take away our freedom to choose. People may try to harm us, and Satan will try to destroy us, but God is our security. When we follow His voice, nothing can succeed at knocking us off course. He truly makes a spiritual feast for us of the blessings of peace, hope, and joy.

Life is a journey filled with hills and valleys. There are rocky slopes and vast canyons to cross, but we don't have to travel them alone. The Good Shepherd is pursuing us with love beyond our ability to comprehend.

Gratitude, Peace, Hope, and Joy

I had a friend a few years ago. He and his family found themselves in a rough situation as his job situation dissolved before his eyes. His wife was pregnant and they had two other kids. In addition to that, he had an accident that landed him in the trauma center for a bit over a month.

He called me one day asking for my husband, who was out of town. We spoke for a few moments, and I read him an article I had written regarding gratitude, peace, and hope. He said it helped him refocus and gave him the perspective he needed in the middle of a place that was darker than he had imagined. We helped with the family and brought the wife to the hospital to see him when we could, but for the most part, he was alone in that place, and he found his way, through gratitude, to see and embrace hope.

Life dramatically changed for this man and his family, but there was a peace and a joy about him that was unmistakable. He no longer saw what they had lost, but instead, he looked at what they had.

Sometimes, we need to let go of what we thought was irreplaceable.

Maybe the dream you have won't come to fruition. Maybe God has a different plan than you have. It's not an easy thing to hear, but in the end, the plan of God is worth the journey through the heartache.

Gratitude in the midst of overwhelming challenges can seem elusive. But gratitude is the basis for peace and hope regardless of the circumstances. Gratitude has been at the core of my healing, I have received God's grace and mercy amid both success and deep, invasive grief. I have found hope and peace beyond my ability to explain or even comprehend.

Years ago, our lives were full and active. We had teenage foster kids and my husband was a builder. We were building a house on thirty-seven acres of land with a lake; life was perfect until the day of Marvin's first heart attack. He was forty years old and I had two kids in school.

Six years later, when my oldest was a senior just graduating from high school and planning on going to Pepperdine in the fall, Marvin had his ninth, and final, heart attack. We were selling our house and moving out to Whidbey Island, off the west coast. The day before our home sold, Marvin passed away. I ended up staying where we were living, and to say that life for our family and particularly for me had been wholly overturned is an understatement.

I knew that God is faithful; I had often said it to others. But it was hard to open my mind and heart at that moment to receive from God. Sometimes we hang on so tightly to what we hope for that we cannot see God's gifts of grace, mercy, peace, and hope. It can be hard to be grateful for where we are when our plans and expectations for our lives are so vastly different from God's.

But God... When we think we have no capacity left, He helps us to allow gratitude to supplant grief, bitterness, anger, and resentment. Through gratitude, He gives us the grace to release, let go, forgive, and heal a broken heart. God is faithful.

Only through gratitude can we understand a microcosm of just how faithful He is. Of course, we only see God's working hands in our lives through colored lenses. But gratitude allows us to see His love and grace more clearly. Peace and hope are the byproducts of gratitude, not the other way around.

The root of gratitude for Christ's followers is Jesus Christ Himself. In all He has done, He portrays the love and faithfulness of God. Jesus left His place in heaven and came to Earth, taking on human flesh, and chose to be a reflection of our Heavenly Father. He gave His life for all of humanity's sins. He chose to be the sacrifice, reconciling us with God. His love was so great that He didn't leave us alone but sent the Holy Spirit to guide and comfort us. He gives us strength, wisdom, and grace when we need it the most, as long as we are willing to hear His still, small voice.

If God did nothing more than what He has already done, we have plenty of reasons to be grateful.

Reflections

- Will you today stop and take a new look at Psalm 23?

- Will you consider it a daily prayer of love, commitment, and celebration rather than held for special occasions?

- What have you learned from your grief and how can that give you compassion for those around you?

8

RESTORATION

There are far, far better things ahead than
any we leave behind.

–C.S. Lewis

We often get weary in our challenges, and it can be tempting to quit or give up. It can feel like it's just too hard to keep going. But even when we are willing to try to tough it out, we need God to give us a new perspective. We all need to remember that we have everything we need inside of us and around us. When we have God as our partner, He shares the journey with us, inspiring, empowering, and keeping us close to His heart.

Paul says this in 1 Corinthians 1:

Just think—you don't need a thing, you've got it all! All God's gifts are right in front of you as you wait expectantly for our Master Jesus to arrive on the scene for the Finale. And not only that, but God himself is right alongside to keep you steady and on track until things are all wrapped up by Jesus. God, who got you started in this spiritual adventure, shares with us the life of his Son and our Master Jesus. He will never give up on you. Never forget that. (v. 7–9, MSG)

To live our lives, we don't need to depend on our own strength, wit, or wisdom. We usually wish that we could know all the details. I can relate to questions like, *"When will this end?" "What value is there in the challenge I'm going through today?"* and *"What does God want from me anyway?"* We sometimes feel like we are out of strength and anything else we need.

Oh yes, I can relate. I have asked these very questions of God.

In looking for answers, I came across Micah. You may be familiar with the NIV version of Micah 6:8, as I was, *"And what does the Lord require of you? To act justly and to love mercy and to walk humbly with your God."*

The Message Translation says it in words that resonate with me.

*But he's already made it plain how to live, what
to do,*

   what God is looking for in men and women.

*It's quite simple: Do what is fair and just to your
neighbor,*

   be compassionate and loyal in your love,

   And don't take yourself too seriously—

   Take God seriously (Micah 6:8, MSG).

God is not asking us to do things that are complicated
—His requirements are simple. God doesn't need us to
carry the whole world; He's already doing that. He
doesn't even expect us to carry our world; trying to carry
things that are outside of our control will weigh us down.
He says that we should be fair and just; when we fall
short, we should humbly go to God and own it. Be
compassionate and loyal in your love; when there is no
compassion in us, we need to go to God and own it.
Above all don't take yourself too seriously—take God
very seriously.

Humbly owning our sins and our lack before God
means that we are not justifying ourselves. We are not
trying to hide from Him, and we are not blaming others
when we are wrong. We are simply going to Him and
humbly asking Him to forgive us, and asking Him to be
strong in us when we are weak. We are asking for His
grace so we can again be fair and just to our neighbors.

We are asking Him to rise in us with His compassion, His loyalty in our love to all, even the unlovable.

We need to learn to take ourselves at face value: our weaknesses, strengths, mistakes, successes, and failures. The beauty in that is that we know for certain that God knows it all and loves us anyway. He desires to lift us and be our provision. Far from being disappointed with us, He wants us to acknowledge our weaknesses so that He can show Himself strong in us.

Above all else, we can take God seriously. Even when your nerves are frazzled and raw, and you can't imagine what it would take to respond with peace, joy, or love, God has offered to be there in that to enable you. Take His promise seriously.

Stop and do a reset. Humbly go to God and say, *"There is not enough of me. I need your help. I need you."* In the name of Jesus, there is more power than we can imagine. In His name, there is abundant strength, healing, and grace. God has a plan and purpose for your life. Be determined to ask for forgiveness and grace, and look to God to blaze your trail!

When we are willing to stop and listen, He will show us the next step in His plan. The plan is much bigger than you or me, but we have our place in it. God is looking at the big picture. We tend to see the small space directly in front of us, but God knows that just as today will pass, so too will the challenge pass. We will be stronger if we go through our days looking to God for that strength.

Resilience

Emotional resilience is an often overlooked factor in recovering from grief. Being emotionally resilient is having the ability to bounce back after a terrible loss. Those who are resilient have learned that grief doesn't have to take the power to be free. It doesn't have to take your joy. The choice to relinquish joy, peace, and freedom because of grief or suffering is just that—a choice.

Being resilient requires that we learn to overwrite the wrong things we have learned in the past with the truth from God's Word, look for the gifts in any situation He allows to come our way, adopt an optimistic way of looking at our lives, and use the mistakes that we have made as learning experiences. It requires that we don't allow ourselves to believe that we are victims of our circumstances. It requires that we take responsibility for our attitudes and actions instead of making excuses for them.

There are a few steps that you can take to help build your emotional resilience. Each one can be a part of growing through your grief to reach the restoration that God has for you on the other side.

First, talk to yourself. You might be thinking that sounds like a crazy idea. But the truth is that we are all talking to ourselves, even if we aren't fully aware of it, all the time. So pay attention to the words you say to yourself. The Bible calls this *"taking every thought captive"* (2 Cor. 10:5, ESV). When you realize that the words you're saying to yourself are thoughts that send you into a downward spiral, stop them. The best antidote for words that bring despair is words that bring hope. Memorize a few Scriptures that bring hope to your heart. When you feel yourself slipping into a dark place in your mind, take the dark thoughts captive by repeating the Scriptures to yourself. Naming things for which you are grateful has a way of changing your perspective from dark to light.

A friend of mine struggled profoundly with fear. She decided that she should begin to take her thoughts captive using Scripture, so she memorized several verses about fear. Every time she felt herself beginning to be overwhelmed by fearful thoughts, she repeated these verses to herself, out loud if possible, until her thoughts stopped racing and her heart stopped pounding. The monologue that plays inside of our heads will influence our emotions and our actions. Remember, there is power in the Word of God.

Create small victories and repetitive positive actions in your life. Each time you do a new thing, something you've not had to do since your journey with grief started, recognize that you did it. You met the challenge, maybe unwillingly, but you still did it.

Maybe you just had to deal with the first tax return on your own, or you needed to set up an internet router for yourself. Maybe the challenge is physical therapy to help your body heal, or counseling to help your heart heal. Each step you take down the road, while it may not feel good, is a success. Celebrate it as such.

Recognize how far you've come. It's important to realize how far you've come. Celebrate the progress you've made on your journey through grief. Perhaps you don't feel that you've made progress. But you're on Chapter 8 of a book about recovering from grief; even that is progress!

Practice gratitude daily. It's not easy to be grateful when all you feel is pain. But gratitude will punch holes in the darkness of your pain and allow little lights to shine through. Remembering with gratitude is a key to emotional resilience.

Louis LaGrand wrote in 2011:

Review each day for the good things that happened—an old friend called, you had great energy and a good night's sleep for a change, you got a raise in pay, your computer is working well, your friend brought over a great meal, etc.—and fully immerse yourself in the good feelings. This is sound mental health in the making. (p. 56)

Gratitude Is a Choice

I love the book by Ann Voskamp, *One Thousand Gifts*. The book is about gratitude, the need to have a grateful heart in the difficult seasons of our lives as well as the wonderfully scrumptious days of love and laughter. She wrote about having a gratitude journal. This idea of a journal to record what we are grateful for is a treasured tool for many that I know. There is something essential about taking the time to write the words of gratitude down. Writing makes those thoughts tangible.

It's imperative that we acknowledge the good, be grateful for the challenges, and treasure the things that really matter. We can be grateful to see God's finger-prints all over our lives, knowing He is there. Maybe He is walking side by side with us, or maybe it's a day that He's carrying us. Either way, we know He's there.

But there is an enemy of our hearts. His focus is to steal, kill, and destroy; and he's good at it. If he can't kill us, he does his best to sideline us, and steal our joy and purpose. Satan tries to attack our standing with God and those around us, keeping us isolated and adding a little despair and pain.

Stealing our hope is a great prize for Satan. But there

is an unlikely weapon that Satan can't defeat—gratitude. When our focus is on God and understanding really who God is and our relationship to Him, we become grateful.

When we come to understand that in the good or in the devastatingly tough times, God will provide what we need to get through to the other side. We have to make a choice though. We have to determine where we will focus our thoughts, emotions, actions, and energy. When we choose to find the things we are grateful for, it changes the trajectory of our thinking, ultimately altering our emotions and actions.

It is a choice to ask God to help you with an attitude of gratitude. Write down 10 things for which you are grateful. If that isn't enough to make a difference in how you feel, then write 20 things. Write things you are grateful for until gratefulness takes over. At that point, the battle for your attitude is won, at least for the moment. You may have to do this exercise daily until it becomes a habit to look for the good, but changing our perspective to gratitude helps us not only face today with a richer view of life, but also look to tomorrow and the future with excitement, hope, and passion!

When we are determined to find what we can be grateful for and list them on paper, we have a history lesson we can remember. I have looked back in my journals to my gratitude list, and I am amazed at the times of great struggle that I came through. Back then those challenges seemed like mountains. Now they look like foothills. I am grateful.

I have to say that, although I don't want to go through them again, with God walking me through those places—and sometimes carrying me—I am better for them. I am a different person than I would have otherwise been because of how I viewed the situation. Being grateful to God and the people He had traveling through my life with me at those key times gave me the ability to be better instead of bitter.

Satan would like us to be defeated, but gratitude provides healing and strength. Gratitude determines where our eyes land: on God and others, or us.

Gratitude takes us outside of ourselves and allows us to see that there is a bigger picture than ourselves. We can look at those around us. We are able to see the needs of others and perhaps see the ways that we can bring hope and encouragement to them. Perhaps a smile, a hot meal, or just time to be heard. It's like paying it forward. Then they have the same opportunity to help someone else.

There are times I'll do something for someone, and when they ask what they can do or what I need, I say: *"Pass it on, do the same for someone else."* It's like putting an extra tool in their toolkit they didn't have: teaching some of the nuts and bolts of being grateful.

God gives us a bevy of tools and resources to

traverse this life with strength, peace, and joy. Gratitude is one of those tools.

King David, who knew both great success and extreme tragedy in his life, says, *"Accept my grateful thanks and teach me Your desires"* (Psalm 119:108, TLB). He was known for his gratitude to God, his Heavenly Father. He danced and sang in thanksgiving in the streets. He allowed everyone to participate. He made gratitude contagious, rich in experience, and full of joy. Some days a thankful heart is easier to unearth than others. Gratitude is a choice. It is intentional. It is a determination to be better and not bitter. Today can you start your gratitude list? Start by writing five things, then five more. You will be amazed when you do.

The Rest of the Story

In the 'Introduction,' I spoke about an episode where God and I wrestled over the hospital bed of my three-year-old daughter. As she lay there, wrapped in padding to prevent her bleeding to death, I had my own Gethsemane moment. I had to say, *"Not my will, but Yours."* When I was weak, the Holy Spirit in me became my strength.

As she lay on the hospital bed, the doctor gave us little to no medical hope for her recovery. The medication for this disease was worse than the disease itself.

Before my daughter, no one had recovered in under two years without significant medication. But test after test, day by day, week after week, for three months, she got better and better. Finally, the doctor pronounced her fully recovered, although there was no medical or scientific explanation for it. Well, there was no explanation other than a miracle.

But there was more accomplished than just her recovery. Marvin worked in a ministry, and in that ministry was a very special young man, Michael, who had become like part of our family. He was a little rough around the edges, and he loved taking things to the limit. Michael loved our daughter so much that he made a deal with God. He promised that if God healed her, he would accept Jesus as his Savior.

He started a *"miracle chart"* that he posted in our kitchen. Every day, when the results came from her blood count test, he wrote it on the chart. A few months later, he put the last test result, the one that prompted the doctor to call her recovery a miracle, on the chart. Then he said to God, *"Well, you did your part, so I'm sure not going to back out on my part."* God's plan was to heal our little girl but to do it in a way that would forever change Michael, as well as several others who saw God at work in the circumstances. All of these people's lives were affected by her recovery. Once I came to a place of peace inside, God was able to touch the lives of many people using something that was undeniably a heart-wrenching circumstance for us.

Decades later, I went to Michael's funeral. He was in his 40s when he was killed in a motorcycle accident. The Naval Chaplain told me that Michael had touched lives for God that he as a Chaplain never could.

My daughter is now in her 40s with two teenage boys. But that one circumstance when she was three had an incredibly positive ripple effect that I would never have considered when I was in the middle of my trouble. At that point, I couldn't see what God was doing. I just knew that if I believed that God was in control and He had our best interest in His plan, then I would have peace. I did, even when I didn't think I could; I had more peace than I could explain or understand.

In 2 Corinthians, Paul tells us God is listening. He is there in the midst of everything: all the things that could go right and all that could go wrong. He is with us in all of it.

Companions as we are in this work with you, we beg you, please don't squander one bit of this marvelous life God has given us. God reminds us, I heard your call in the nick of time; The day you needed me, I was there to help. Well, now is the right time to listen, the day to be helped. Don't put it off; don't frustrate God's work by showing up late, throwing a question mark over everything we're doing. Our work as God's servants gets vali-

dated—or not—in the details. People are watching us as we stay at our post, alertly, unswervingly . . . in hard times, tough times, bad times; when we're beaten up, jailed, and mobbed; working hard, working late, working without eating; with pure heart, clear head, steady hand; in gentleness, holiness, and honest love; when we're telling the truth, and when God's showing his power; when we're doing our best setting things right; when we're praised, and when we're blamed; slandered, and honored; true to our word, though distrusted; ignored by the world, but recognized by God; terrifically alive, though rumored to be dead; beaten within an inch of our lives, but refusing to die; immersed in tears, yet always filled with deep joy; living on handouts, yet enriching many; having nothing, having it all (6:1–10, MSG).

Sometimes in our lives, we will have trouble; that's just the way life is. It is not what happens to us that means so much. It's what we do with what happens to us that means everything in the world.

Don't quit now; there is so much more ahead!

Reflections

- Do you have a quiet place where you can go, even if only for a few minutes, to intentionally stop and connect to God regardless of what's happening?

- How can you begin to keep a record of the things you're grateful for today?

CONCLUSION

As you continue on the road of grieving, my hope for you is that you will keep running through your pain toward God. He's the only One who can make your heart whole again. I pray that you have found hope in these pages—hope that life will be good again, that your heart will heal, and that God has never and will never leave you.

Anger, fear, and disappointment are weapons that Satan uses to discourage us when life is hard. He wants us to isolate ourselves from God and the people who love us. But God isn't going to walk away from you! Even when He doesn't answer our prayer the way we wish He had, He still cares for us, protects us, and walks with us. His love for us is amazing, and life's most difficult situations can't separate us from Him.

Romans 8 says it this way:

For I am convinced that neither death nor life, neither angels nor principalities, neither the present nor the future, nor any powers, neither height nor depth, nor anything else in all creation, will be able to separate us from the love of God that is in Christ Jesus our Lord (v.38–39, NIV).

Learning to express gratitude to God even in the hardest experiences of our lives will help us to see our reality through the lens of eternity instead of with our temporal eyes. Gratitude will enable us to give others the comfort that they need, which will in return provide comfort and healing to our own hearts. One of the ways that God heals our hearts is by helping us get our eyes off of ourselves and help those around us.

Healing is a journey. Along the way, God provides us with others to support us. Don't be afraid to lean on the people God has put into your life to help you. Friends, family, prayer partners, counselors, spiritual leaders, and small groups can all play an integral role in our healing.

This world is at war, and we have an enemy who would love to destroy us! The weapons God gives us—love, compassion, and gratitude—are not the weapons our flesh wants to fight with. But God knows the battle plan! He has already won, and we are walking in His victory when we use His weapons.

God will guide us. He is our shepherd—our Good

Shepherd. Peace, joy, and hope are the outflow of gratitude in our hearts. Choosing to take our thoughts captive when they are counterproductive to healing, celebrating our forward action, remembering with gratitude, and recognizing how far we've come are ways to help yourself be more emotionally resilient. Learn to change your thinking—override the thought processes that come naturally to you with the truth from God's Word whenever necessary.

And above all, practice gratitude and love, our strongest weapons to defeat the enemy.

One Last Reminder...

We can win the battle waged against our hearts and minds because of Jesus' death and resurrection. We gain strength and confidence in remembering that God was faithful in the past and He will be again.

Our attitude determines everything about us and how we view life. Our perspective will determine how we looked at the world and our circumstances.

Even today I still work on my attitude of gratitude, remembering how incredibly good God has been to me.

Revelation 12:11 says, *"And they have conquered him by the blood of the Lamb and by the word of their testimony, for they loved not their lives even unto death."*

We know how the war ends. God wins, and we will win with Him. Let's go out there and live like it!

RESOURCES

- Allender, D. B. (2021). Redeeming heartache: how past suffering reveals our true calling. (Kindle). Zondervan.
- The Amplified Bible. (1958). Zondervan.
- Anderson, J. (2014, March). Lights wink. All My Loose Ends. http://allmylooseends.com/2014/03/lights-wink
- Cacciatore, J. (2017). Bearing the unbearable : love, loss, and the heartbreaking path of grief. Wisdom Publications.
- Champ, L. (2021, June 1). 6 signs you haven't grieved properly. Red Online.
- https://www.redonline.co.uk/wellbeing/a36590728/ unresolved-grief/
- Collins, J. M. (2021, May 21). Who was Sedona, Arizona's Sedona Schnebly? Jan MacKell Collins.
- https://janmackellcollins.wordpress.com/2021/05/21/ who-was-sedona-arizonas-sedona-schnebly/
- Evans, K., & Sullivan, J. M. (1995). Treating addicted survivors of trauma. Guilford Press.
- G5015–tarassō–strong's Greek lexicon (nkjv). (n.d.). Blue Letter Bible.
- https://www.blueletterbible.org/lexicon/g5015/nkjv/tr/0-1

- Goodreads librarians group. (2015, March 29). Goodreads. https://www.goodreads.com/topic/show/2272421-winnie-the-pooh

- Grief. (2019, January 9). Wikimedia Foundation. https://en.wikipedia.org/wiki/Grief

- Guthrie, N. (2009). Hearing Jesus Speak into Your Sorrow. (Kindle). Tyndale House Publishers.

- Hairston, S. (2019, July 11). How Grief Shows Up In Your Body. WebMD. https://www.webmd.com/special-reports/grief-stages/20190711/how-grief-affects-your-body-and-mind

- Healthy grieving. (2020). Counseling Center at the University of Washington. https://www.washington.edu/counseling/resources-for-students/healthy-grieving/

- Henry Wadsworth Longfellow Quotes. (n.d.). Brainy Quotes. https://www.brainyquote.com/quotes/henry_wadsworth_longfello_139003

- The Holy Bible: English Standard Version. (n.d.). American Bible Society.

- Holy Bible: NIV: New International Version. (1973). Christian Media Bibles.

- Jaju, B., Phiske, M., Lade, N., & Jerajani, H. (2009). Hematohidrosis–a rare clinical phenomenon. Indian Journal of Dermatology, 54(3), 290. https://doi.org/10.4103/0019-5154.55645

- James, J. W., & Friedman, R. (2009). The grief recovery handbook, 20th anniversary expanded edition: the action program for moving beyond death, divorce, and other losses including health, career, and faith. Harper Perennial.

- Kubler-Ross, E., & Kessler, D. (2021, March 15). Grief quotes celebrating the life of someone who passed away. Everyday Power. https://everydaypower.com/grief-quotes/
- LaGrand, L. (2011). Healing grief, finding peace: daily strategies for grieving and growing. (Kindle). Sourcebooks.
- Lewis, C. (1961). A grief observed. Harper-Collins. https://portalconservador.com/livros/C-S-Lewis-A-Grief-Observed.pdf
- Lewis, C. S., & Hooper, W. (2006). Collected letters. vol. 3, Narnia, Cambridge and joy 1950-1963. Harpercollins Publishers.
- Lilius, J., Kanov, J., Dutton, J., Worline, M., & Maitlis, S. (2011). Compassion revealed: what we know about compassion at work (and where we need to know more). Oxford University Press.
- Miller, B. (2019, November 21). Devotional--I walked a mile with pleasure. Utica United Methodist Church. https://uticaumc.org/2019/11/21/devotional-i-walked-a-mile-with-pleasure
- Peterson, E. H. (2004). The Message Bible. Navpress.
- Programs for bereaved/grieving parents & families - the kindness project. (n.d.). Miss Foundation. https://www.missfoundation.org/kindness-project/

- Ten Boom, C. (1984). Clippings from my notebook : writings and sayings collected. World Wide Publications.
- Trauma and Shock. (2021). American Psychological Association. https://www.apa.org/topics/trauma
- Types of Grief and Loss. (2019, May 1). Elizz. https://elizz.com/caregiver-resources/types-of-grief-and-loss
- Understanding the Fog of Grief: No, You Aren't Losing Your Mind. (2020, January 16). Batchelor Brothers. https://batchelorbrothers.com/blogs/blog-entries/3/Batchelor-Brothers-News-Events/92/Understanding-the-Fog-of-Grief-No-You-Aren-t-Losing-Your-Mind.html
- What is grief? (2016, October 19). Mayo Clinic. https://www.mayoclinic.org/patient-visitor-guide/support-groups/what-is-grief

ABOUT THE AUTHOR

From the age of 28, Deb King's mission statement has been "To teach people how to reach their God-given potential through the power of Christ." She has applied that mission statement to her personal relationships, her business, and her recovery journey.

Deb has always had a passion for helping people get through hard places to dream of finding peace amidst excruciating pain, heartache, and joy. It is a gift to find hope in the valley and mountain top. Deb and her husband Marvin had a few hundred teenage emergency shelter foster children. She found it incredible to see the light go on in their heads and hearts when the kids dared to dream and believe they could thrive, regardless of their pain and suffering.

Being a recovering alcoholic of 43 years, Deb has had the opportunity to work with many whose actions needed to grieve the choices and consequences of their decisions and who found the shared experience, strength, and hope that could choose to thrive on the journey of sobriety.

I often asked the person I was meeting, "If money wasn't an object, what would you dream that you would want to be or do? Follow-up questions always were what is stopping you; Can you stop for a moment and allow yourself to dream? God has a plan for your life. Are you willing to dream and believe you can achieve your dream regardless of the obstacles?" She still asks those questions of those she meets today.

Deb is a two-time widow, Marvin had nine heart attacks in 6 years before his passing, and Steve had a nine-month hard fought battle with cancer. Unfortunately, she is no stranger to loss, her mother passed away a few years before her father passed, and her Father-in-law passed just nine months before her husband.

She has two biological daughters and five grandchildren who are the delight of her heart! With both of her husbands they blended their families and experienced the challenges and joys that can come with it.

Deb has been a business owner, operator, and investor, for 35 years in various industries.

She understands the loss of family and dreams and has had life take a 90-degree or 280-degree turn from what she hoped for or expected. Yet, there have been failures and successes over the years, and one thing is evident in her story, God is Faithful.

I sincerely hope this book has been a blessing to you. If so, please review it on Amazon so that more who need to hear the message will be able to hear it. I'd also love to connect with you.

Find me online by scanning the QR code below or visit the website at www.ehtftc.com to read and listen to weekly inspirational and thought provoking content.

f facebook.com/everyonehasthefreedomtochoose

twitter.com/ehtftc

instagram.com/ehtftc

youtube.com/@EHTFTC

BOOKS BY THE SAME AUTHOR

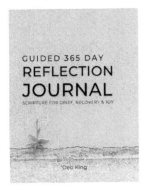